The Book of
Williton

A Portrait of the Parish

Michael Williams

HALSGROVE

First published in Great Britain in 2001

British Library Cataloguing-in-Publication Data
A CIP record for this title is available from the British Library

ISBN 1 84114 1151

HALSGROVE
PUBLISHING, MEDIA AND DISTRIBUTION

Halsgrove House
Lower Moor Way
Tiverton, Devon EX16 6SS
Tel: 01884 243242
Fax: 01884 243325
email: sales@halsgrove.com
website: http://www.halsgrove.com

Frontispiece photograph: *George Chidgey and Ted Stevens astride a Rudge Whitworth motorcycle during the 1930s.*

Printed and bound in Great Britain by Bookcraft Ltd, Midsomer Norton.

FOREWORD

by Ralph White (Liddymore Farm)

I am sure that those of us who were born in Williton and those who have come from away to make their home here have at some time wondered about the origin and development of the village and its environs. For providing many of the answers to our questions we can thank Michael Williams, who has taken the time to research and record much of Williton's past through to the 21st century. Among other things, we are able to see how Williton has gradually changed from a predominantly agricultural community to a village in which few members of the growing population have any involvement, directly or indirectly, with the land.

Over the last 50 years I have witnessed the demise of at least five agricultural holdings within the parish and with them have gone the blacksmith, wheelwright, saddler and miller, to name but a few. We are aware that change is constantly taking place as businesses and organisations come and go, and housing estates envelop more and more of the surrounding fields. Shop fronts change, trees are cut down and occasionally a house is demolished – already Kebby's Farm and Tommy Bellamy's shop are becoming distant memories. Fortunately we have had three generations of the Hole family living in Williton whose business was photography and through them we have been left a wonderful visual record of the village and the life of its community covering well over a century. To have these photographs of the past put together with contemporary photographs helps us to appreciate the extent of the changes that have occurred even in comparatively recent times. I wonder what changes will take place in the future for another historian to record?

Blacksmiths at work at the turn of the last century.

Just some of the many old thatched cottages which have long since disappeared in Williton. The sign above the doorway in this photograph of High Street by H.H. Hole reads: 'J. Bevin, Grocer and Boot Dealer. Licensed to sell Tobacco.' Down the road is the garage and the sign on the nearby wall low down is advertising 'Mobiloils', whilst the pump provides motorists with a supply of Pratt's petrol.

Orchard Wyndham, dating from some time between 1860 and 1890. (Courtesy James Date Archive)

CONTENTS

An evocative photograph of the Railway Hotel from the studio of H.H. Hole. It is dated between 1867 and 1873 and shows a horse-drawn vehicle signwritten with the name of the establishment.

The spire seen in this early photograph by James Date is thought to have been lost during a gale c.1870.
(Courtesy James Date Archive)

Acknowledgements

In putting together this record, I am grateful to the many people who have assisted with material and information. Some of the information cannot be verified, or date accuracy guaranteed, but I have made every effort to record a picture of Williton that I hope will be of interest to many. Some of the photographs are from collections and I would like to thank all who have lent them for publication. They include: Air Pic, D. Clarke, D. Langdon, F.J. Hutchings, Edward Martin, Mrs H. Tennant, Mrs M. Clarke, David Jefferies, Mrs J. Barnes, Mrs M. Milnes, D. Beach, D.W. Sully, M. Chapman, W. Matravers, P. Armstrong, Ben Gliddon, Mrs M. Slade, Mrs A. Scrace, Mrs M. Binding, Mrs V. Buller, R. White, K.W. Towells, N.E. Pullin, Mr and Mrs R. Atherton, Mrs V. Pope, D.J. Sully, M.H. Jones, Mrs V. Chibbett, 'Kwinty', Mr and Mrs K. Bishop, Mrs Lee Ackland, M. Ashman, Mrs P. Morrison, Mrs V. Bond, Mrs A. Palmer, Mrs M. Steer, Mrs J. Hill, Mrs V. Chidgey and Mrs Lyddon.

Particular thanks for assistance are due to: Mr P. Towells, Mr F. Morgan, Dr K. Wyndham and David Gliddon. Thanks also to the Somerset Record Office and the editor of the *West Somerset Free Press*, together with very special thanks for expert advice and assistance from Mr and Mrs M. Chidgey, who have made a substantial contribution to this book. My sincere thanks to all who have assisted me in preparing this record.

Michael Williams

An early aerial shot of Williton. Evidence can still be seen of the ancient strip-field system in the top left-hand corner of the picture.

Below and left: *The horseman seen below is facing towards the original road into Williton before Highbridge was built. A short distance along this road a lane leads to Egrove Farm* (left), *where a mill operated intermittently from 1275 onwards. An iron wheel from Egrove Mill is stored as a museum piece spare at Combe Sydenham Country Park Estate.*

Right: *The floods of October 1924. With a long and varied history, Williton has many legends and stories attached to it. One of the best known perhaps is that of Mother Shipton, who said famously: 'Watchet and Doniford both shall drown and Williton become the seaport town'. A famous witch and prophetess, Mother Shipton was much travelled, as it is said that she had a cave which can still be visited at Knaresborough in Yorkshire.*

Left: *Getting the feel of any location is often best achieved on foot and beginning, in Williton, at or near Orchard Wyndham before exploring the village itself, it soon becomes apparent that water from the surrounding area flows freely around and through the settlement on its way to the sea. There is evidence of several water wheels in the parish, one of which – a complete overshot wheel – still exists at Orchard Mill. Not far away was Bridge Mill* (pictured here). *Four further water wheels appear to have existed – at Egrove Farm, Bridge Street, Catwell and Station Road.*

Right: *Further exploration of the parish on foot and passing Egrove Farm leads us to Doniford and its beach, pictured here. Standing near the mouth of the 'Swilley' it is easy to imagine it as a site where the Danes beached their ships and crept inshore through the valley toward the main Williton settlement near the Bury, only to be met at Battlegore by defenders of the settlement. Battlegore is also reputed to have been the scene of a famous duel between the devil and the giant, who issued his challenge from the Quantocks.*

Chapter One

A Brief Overview of the Parish

Over the years the name Williton has been variously recorded as: Willetton, Willeton, Welletone, Wylton, Wyllyton and Gillitone, to name but a few. There are no doubt other spellings derived from the (River) Willite which is said to have given Williton its name. References to Battlegore take us back to AD918 and we are reminded that attacks from the sea by Danes were of serious concern to communities along the coast. The name Battlegore (which is thought to mean battle on a triangular or wedge-shaped area) and Danesfield are still much used. Battlegore was indicated on the map included in the 1907 official guide for Watchet, Williton and Washford and a triangular field marked Biddlegore can be seen on the Wyndham Estate map.

In 1086 at the time of the Domesday Book, Carhampton, Cannington and Williton (Hundreds) formed a single estate of Royal Demesne but by the 12th century the Manor of Williton had passed into the hands of Richard Fitz Urse and later to his son Reynold (or Reginald). Reginald Fitz Urse (one of the Becket murderers) divided the manor in two, and half was passed to his brother Robert (c.1180) and the other half to the Knights of St John of Jerusalem. The descended Manor of Williton is that half of the manor which passed to Robert Fitz Urse and which, in turn, was later divided into two estates known as Williton Fulford and Williton Hadley. The Fulford Estate was sold to Sir John Wyndham in 1616 and in 1710 the Hadley Estate was purchased from Alexander Luttrell by Sir William Wyndham.

A model of a 16th-century almshouse.

The site of the original manor house, in which Reginald Fitz Urse spent a number of his childhood years, has been recorded by means of a sketch map assembled from early records printed in the book *The Parish of St Peter Williton*, and the site of the manor house is indicated as abutting the river to the south of St Peter's Church and Cottages.

Little in the way of local records exists of the period 1200–1500, but it is assumed that Williton experienced conditions similar to other parts of the country and lost a third of its population to the plague in 1348. Preceding this the first Parliament to include commoners had been called in 1265. Discontent among labourers was starting to express itself and there were calls for direct payments for services so that the populace could have more control over their lives and reap the rewards of greater effort. Following the plague a shortage of labour paved the way for an era in which those with little or no freedom previously could now demand higher prices for their labours. Feudal estates were broken up and freemen purchased their own parcels of land and became lords of their own destinies for the first time.

It has been suggested that the street layout of Williton originated as crossroads and with little imagination this seems likely with the east and west intersections at different points being marked by Lower Cross and Higher Cross. White Cross seems to have marked the eastern end of the village and Water Cross the northern end. Chapel Cross was most probably the parish cross around which most of the early village developed.

The early development of Williton took place mainly at its western end, but properties bearing the dates 1607 and 1624 can be seen in Long Street, the date 1616 in Robert Street, and a rebuilt date of 1724 in Half Acre. They may not be the oldest in these areas. Construction of the old properties was with cob, a roof of thatch and a stone floor, and this still

Swillbridge House, early-19th century. (Courtesy James Date Archive)

Until the 19th century the main coastal route from Bridgwater to Williton and beyond passed through Doniford which at one time was the largest farm holding in the parish. Other activities to have taken place there include lime burning, milling and the collection and drying of Ore weed (seaweed). The present-day road from Rydon to Doniford serves a holiday campsite which in earlier days had been the site of Territorial Regular Army camps. Doniford is also a halt on the West Somerset Railway line.

stands the test of time. At the western end of the village the layout has not altered greatly over the years, so it is still possible to get a feel of how things might have been, with the field known as the Bury, in which ancient sports (including bull fighting) took place, centre stage. To the north of the field in Priest Street there are properties on both sides of the thoroughfare known as Almshouse Lane where once stood the almshouses (built in 1630) – dwellings let at low rates to the poor. Where the Church Room and ATC hut stand now was the site of the Priest's House (rebuilt in 1622), situated at the eastern end of the strip of land known as Priest's Acre, and this latter ended in the area where, in 1907, the new vicarage (now a nursing home) was built.

To the south of the Bury is Bridge Farm and St Peter's Church with cottages to its rear, a little further west one comes to Eastfield House and Orchard Wyndham lodge leading to Orchard Wyndham, and to the north-west is Orchard Mill.

Not far from the Bury and High Cross stood the Coach and Horses which was the the centre of many activities and a resting place for travellers and their mounts. Courts were sometimes held in a part of the premises and nearby stood a single cell lock-up with a grilled window in which arrested persons were held – and oft-times abused by passers-by.

Until the 19th century Williton was reached from the coastal route from Bridgwater that entered the parish (St Decuman's) at Rydon, passing through Doniford to Watchet and then to Williton by Leechway or Liddymore Lane. Access to Williton from the south was limited by very minor lanes but in 1807 a direct road from Taunton was established and the existing minor roads improved. In 1829 a direct line road from St Audries was made into Williton and established what was to become the important thoroughfare of today. As the roads were improved, so a number of the bridges became less important, but the names Fowl Bridge (1492), Highbridge (1438), Little Bridge (1515) and Mamsey remain with us. The bridge carrying the road across the river into Bridge Street was formerly known as Back Street Bridge and the road itself as Back Street or Back Lane. A property lease from a dwelling in this area dated 1744 contains a reference to Gallows Street.

The site of Williton's almshouse/s is not certain, but there is record of a cottage standing on the site of an almshouse in Almshouse Lane on the Wyndham Estate map of 1800–05 (held at the County Record Office). The design and structure of almshouses often represented a very considerable advance in standards, possibly due to the fact that they commonly enjoyed the patronage of wealthy benefactors, after which the buildings were often named. Many well maintained and improved examples still provide good homes and there is a preserved section from a 16th-century terrace of such houses at the Castle Museum in Taunton. Basic human needs were met by earth closets, and water was obtained from wells. The supply was not always clean and cider and beer were sometimes drunk as a means of obtaining a safe beverage. As pumps began to appear, however, the water was less subject to pollution thanks to covers on the wells. Foods eaten by the poor were rye bread, cheese and broths made from scraps of meat, sometimes supplemented with bacon or fish and seasonal apples, etc.

The Wyndham Estate map of 1800–05 confirms that development at the beginning of the 19th century was in the main confined to Shutgate Street (now North Street), Long Street, Priest Street and Bridge Street. The Estate records indicate that at that time Henry Tripp, a barrister, was the farmer responsible for the total management of the landholding. As was the custom, Mr Tripp took on an apprentice whom he trained as his clerk and deputy. This deputy was Mr Thomas Hawkes, who later, with others, established the Williton Auctions. In earlier days he carried out surveys and valuations and was succeeded by his son, another T. Hawkes, who was associated with surveys for railways and later with two other well-known Williton businessmen, Messrs Risdon and Hosegood. It is said that the parasol was introduced into Williton by the wife of Mr Hawkes senr, who was brought from London by her husband to make their home at (85) Long Street.

There were many milestones that punctuated the Victorian era locally, among them the arrival of the railway branch line at Watchet from Taunton in 1862, when a station was also established at Williton. The first edition of the *West Somerset Free Press* was published on 28 July 1860 and an Act of Parliament was passed the following year which was designed to make building sites more readily accessible. Although Williton only benefited slightly from this move, thrifty and generous management by the trustees of the late Earl of Egremont's estate and the kindness of his widowed Countess ensured considerable and noticeable improvements during the ensuing 20 years.

A present-day photograph of the River Willite flowing round to the rear of Church Cottages.

Parish Crosses

Left and below: *The pedestal of Higher Cross at its site on the corner of the Egremont Hotel and preserved in the garden of the NatWest Bank.*

Right: *Chapel Cross. This cross is also just visible between the two trees in the photograph at the top of page 14.*

Above: *The pedestal of Lower Cross, which once stood on Jones' Corner, now in the garden adjoining the NatWest Bank. Unfortunately, no similar trace remains of White Cross.*

Right: *The pedestal of Water Cross which stood originally on a site at Doniford. The tops of all of the crosses have now been lost to decay, vandalism and some traffic damage.*

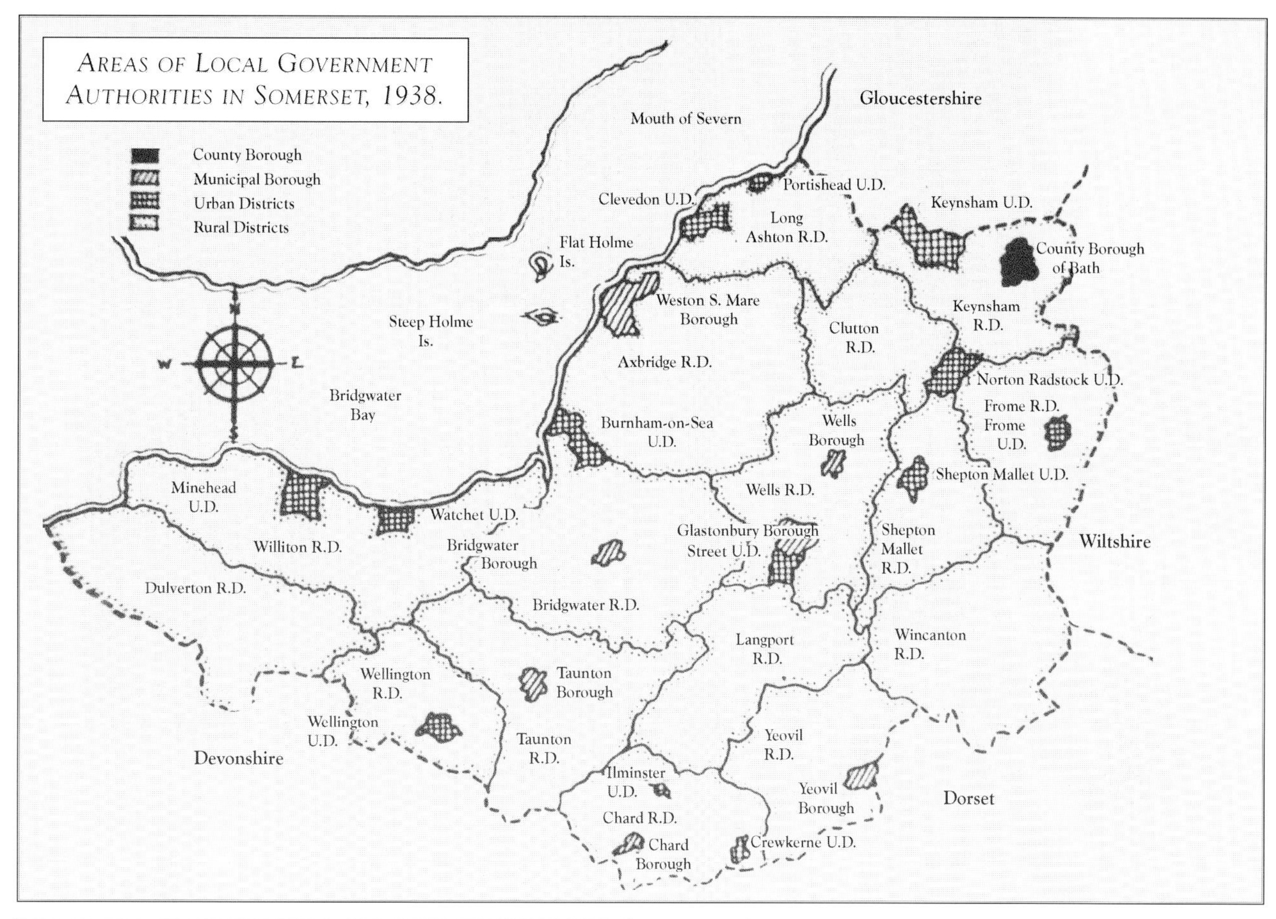

Above: *Council Offices at Williton. Somerset County Council came into being on 1 April 1889 and included 16 urban district councils, 17 rural district councils and 415 parish councils. The parishes of West Somerset are: Bicknoller, Brompton Ralph, Brompton Regis, Brushford, Carhampton, Clatworthy, Crowcombe, Cutcombe, Dulverton, Dunster, East Quantoxhead, Elworthy, Exford, Exmoor, Exton, Holford, Huish Champflower, Kilve, Luccombe, Luxborough, Minehead, Monksilver, Nettlecombe, Oare, Old Cleeve, Porlock, Sampford Brett, Selworthy, Skilgate, Stogumber, Stogursey, Treborough, Timberscombe, Upton, Watchet, West Quantoxhead, Williton, Winsford, Withycombe, Withypool and Hawkridge, and Wootton Courtenay.*

WILLITON: THE CIVIL PARISH

In times of old Williton was a chapter in the ancient parish of St Decuman's but following the Local Government Act of 1894, it became a separate civil parish (1902). The population of the parish of St Decuman's (combined parishes) in 1902 was 3302 and almost a century later the population of Williton (in 1998) was 2410.

The parish of Williton as recorded in Young's guide to the administrative units of England can be summarised as follows: A chapter in the ancient parish of St Decuman's; Separate ecclesiastical parish 1784; Separate civil parish 1902; Local government: Williton Poor Law Union and Rural District Council Parliamentary representation: Bridgwater Division (1918); Rural Deaneries: Dunster 1784–1872, Wiveliscombe 1872–1952, Dunster 1952–73, Quantock 1954–; Ecclesiastical boundary change: 1954.

It is sometimes said that one does not go to Williton but through it. Admittedly, sitting astride the A39 which meets the A358 and having link roads to Watchet and Doniford, this is inevitably often the case, but one soon discovers that for many reasons Williton is more than just a thoroughfare. In ancient times, it was one of the largest settlements in Somerset and more recently has become a seat of local government for the district, with offices at its centre which serve the West Somerset District Council (one of the five areas of Somerset with a second tier of local government).

St Peter's Church with a donkey cart outside, c.1865. (Courtesy James Date Archive)

The church after the loss of its spire. Visible on the right are the cottages where beer was brewed and sold at church ales.

CHAPTER TWO

The Ecclesiastical Parish

ST PETER'S CHURCH

The date of origin of the Parish Church seems in doubt, but St Peter's, which was originally a 'Chapel of Ease' in the parish of St Decuman's, existed at least as far back as the 14th century and at one time had a gallery, stone pulpit and rood screen. The church was rebuilt and enlarged in 1857 and a tracing of an old drawing of the interior (*bottom right*) illustrates the building before enlargement. Inside the church today one can still see the unusual font of local alabaster and windows that have been dedicated as memorials, whilst outside stands the Chapel Cross which is thought to date from the 14th century. Restorations to the church interior took place during 1949 and this work was recorded in the *West Somerset Free Press* on 29 October of that year. A tablet on the west wall of the Sanctuary records the restorations:

The excellent work in
this Sanctuary
was dedicated to the memory
of those who died in
The Second World War
1939–1945
by the Lord Bishop of Bath and Wells
Sunday 5th March 1950

Changes to the interior of the church are currently under consideration so as to meet the requirements of a modern-day house of worship and its congregation.

During the period of elected local government Williton has been served by nine vicars:

S.J. Heathcote 1854–1906
C.W. Heale 1906–17
B.J. Langham 1918–28
A.C. Waggett 1928–45
H. Saxby 1945–52
F.H. Hall 1953–62
A.H. Lovelock 1963–83
J. Andrews 1984–92
R. Allen 1993–

From 1907 the vicars lived in the Vicarage in Priest Street which is now Mamsey House Nursing Home. The Church Room remains in Priest Street and has been updated so as to extend its use and purpose. The present vicar at the time of writing, Reverend Richard Allen, lives in the replacement Vicarage in Bridge Street.

Early references to church music are rare, but mention is made of the existence of a gallery – probably used by a choir or musicians. Singers are mentioned in the 18th century and two instruments recorded in the 19th century, one of which was presented by the Countess of Egremont and the other by the residents of Williton. Mr T. Sparks was organist from 1913 until 1939, and he was followed by his widow Mrs W. Sparks, who continued to play the organ for some time. It seems likely but not certain that the organ was built by a Mr Sparks, who was in the family business as an organ builder. The church organ has been played for many years by Mrs V. Chibbett and Mrs M. Slade. Mr W.H. Ashman served the church as a chorister for 60 years and Mr Reg Sutton for 50 years. Their service is recorded on brass plates in the present choir stalls. Beginning in Parson Heale's time as organ blower Mr Ashman then joined the boy choristers and when his voice broke he stayed on to sing bass under the eye of the late Mr Sid Bellamy.

Church Community

Left: *St Peter's Church Sunday School, c.1946. The teachers at the back are, left to right: Miss M. Davis, Miss M. Ashman, Miss E. Clarke.*

Below: *Williton Church Choir outing, 1920s.*

Below left: *Advertisement for the business of Henry Sparks, whose family were local organ builders and members of the congregation at St Peter's.*

HENRY SPARKS,

ORGAN BUILDER, PIANO-FORTE Tuner, and Repairer of all kinds of Musical Instruments, FORE STREET, WILLITON, returns his sincere thanks to his friends and the public generally, for the kind support accorded him since his commencement in business (now 17 years since), and begs to inform them that he is assisted by his Brothers, William and James Sparks, who with him will still endeavour to maintain the position he has acquired, by continuing to build, tune, and repair, and also to supply all kinds of Musical Instruments, at the lowest possible prices.

All the newest Music, consisting of Sacred Pieces, Songs (Solos, Duets, &c.), Dances, Operas, Instruction Books, &c., supplied at a reduction of from Threepence to Sixpence off the Shilling.--Music to order on same terms.

N.B.—The Organ, Piano-forte, and all Wind and String Instruments taught. Terms on application.

Nativity plays of the 1950s at St Peter's.

Above: *St Peter's Church fête helpers at the Recreation Ground, late 1940s.*

Left: *The cast of* Snow White, *2001.*

Below left: *Mary Slade at the piano for the production.*

Below: *Seven large dwarfs.*

The St Peter's Players presented Snow White and the Seven Dwarfs *as their first presentation in the refurbished Church Room in February 2001. Proceeds were donated to further improvements of the room. The cast, which is pictured centre left, included: Roxanne Langdon, Charlotte Kimberly, Christopher Williams, Andrew Martin, Sarah Thrush, Steve Bailey, Sue Bailey, Lucy Bailey, Harriet Bailey, Rupert Bailey, Colin Tennant, Sally Ann Tennant, William Tennant, Rebecca Tennant, John Tennant, Maureen Wheeler, Jane Ninis, Sally Scyner, Mark Scyner, Trudi Thompson, Sue Withycombe, Jennie Allen, Richard Allen and Pam Allen. Working on the wardrobe were Pam Stephens, Mary Bambridge and Joan Gilham. The prompt was Heather Tennant, scenery was left in the capable hands of Geoff Gilham, the music with Mary Slade and Ken Cook, and in charge of the curtain was Terry Stevens.*

The former Priest Street Vicarage, now extended and known as Mamsey House Nursing Home.

The old Priest's House. A Mr Beare kept a school here in 1802, and it was afterwards occupied by excisemen for several years in succession. Then the house was lived in by Mr James Thristle, and the late Mr John Gliddon went there when he was first married.

Revd C.W. Heale (1906–17).

Revd B.J. Langham (1918–28).

Revd A.C. Waggett (1928–45).

Revd A.H. Lovelock (1963–83).

The Methodist Chapel and schoolroom at Tower Hill.

The chapel builders in 1883.

WILLITON CHAPELS

The long-closed chapel building can still be seen in Catwell where it was converted to two cottages adjoining an existing pair to make a row of four. The original date of the chapel building is in doubt although it is certainly early. Together with Watchet and Stogumber, Williton was one of a group of three jointly administered chapels. Williton's chapel was used for services from 1844 until 1919 and enjoyed a healthy level of attendance by many well-known local people, including Harry Gliddon, Sammy Coles, John Chilcott, the Churchills and J.W. Williams, a local businessman recorded as trading from the County Stores site in 1876 and selling firearms and hardware.

Protestant Nonconformity was introduced in Williton by preachers from Watchet around 1770, but in 1810 the house of Mr and Mrs Stoate (prominent Methodists), on the site of the present Westminster Bank, was used for worship. This continued until 1820 when the first Methodist chapel was built off Fore Street. Sunday School commenced in 1822. The chapel was replaced in 1883 by a splendid building at the bottom of Tower Hill built by J. Chibbett and Sons, local builders of high repute.

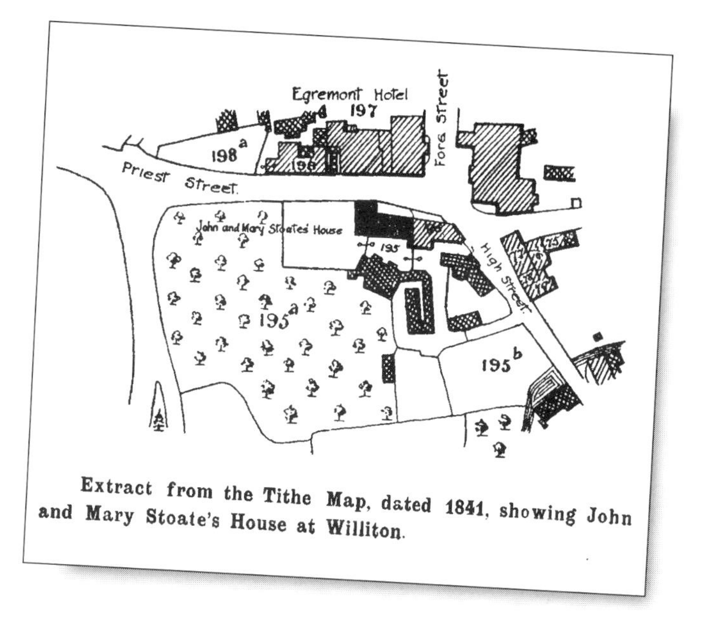

Extract from the Tithe Map, dated 1841, showing John and Mary Stoate's House at Williton.

Above: *Harvest thanksgiving time at the Baptist chapel in Catwell, now converted to cottages. It served as a chapel from 1844–1919.*

Right: *Map from the booklet printed to mark the centenary of Williton Methodist Chapel in 1910 (see over).* (Courtesy James Date Archive)

Below: *The Wesleyan Synod, Exeter District, at Williton, 8 May 1907.*

Centenary Celebration Booklet, 1910

Wesleyan Methodist Church

WILLITON CIRCUIT

Centenary Celebration

1910

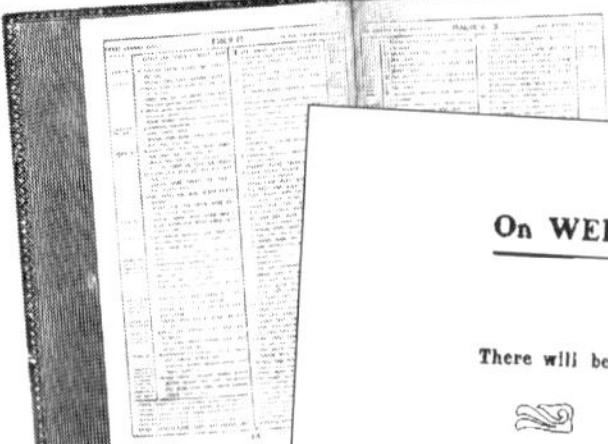

On WEDNESDAY, 23rd MARCH, 1910

The 100th Anniversary of the Licensing of the House of John and Mary Stoate, in Williton, for Public Worship

There will be a **Memorial Service** in the Afternoon at 3.45,

AT THE WESLEYAN CHAPEL, WILLITON,

When a Sermon will be preached by the Rev. E. J. BRAILSFORD, Chairman of the Exeter District.

The Holy Communion will be administered at the close of the Service.

TEA will be provided at 5.30. Tickets 6d. each.

There will be a **Public Meeting** in the Evening at 7 o'clock,

To be presided over by Mr. James Stoate, of Torre.

The Revs. James Finch, G. Adcock, H. Down, and Messrs. James Wood, G. Brown, T. Hosegood, John Hill, B. Gliddon, Wm. Stoate, and the Superintendent Minister of the Circuit will take part.

Singing at both Services by a United Choir, and a Collection will be taken for the Circuit Fund.

The Original Copy of the License and other Historical Documents will be on view after the Service in the Church Parlour. Additions to these solicited.

Chronology of Methodist Events in West Somerset.

1744. Wesley visited Minehead and preached near the sea shore. He was again at Minehead in the following year on his way to Wales.

1790. Methodism introduced into Holnicote and Carhampton by the Taunton preachers.

1790. Williton, Holnicote, and Carhampton appear on the Taunton Plan.

1798. First Quarterly Meeting, held at the Green Dragon, Bilbrook.

1800. First Class formed at Washford.

1810. Mr. Stoate's House, at Williton, Licensed for Methodist Services. The Ministers in the Taunton Circuit at this time were Revs. Wm. Pearson, sen., William Jenkins, and Edward Banks.

1811. Dunster Circuit separated from Taunton.

1811. First Chapel built at Dunster.

1811. First Chapel built at Lower Washford.

1812. Chapel built at Withypool.

1814. Society formed at Roadwater — 16 members.

1816. A Chapel fitted up at Cutcombe.

1820. Washford Class (34) divided—16 meeting at Williton.

1820. First Chapel built at Williton.

1821. Sunday School commenced at Washford.

1822. Sunday School commenced at Williton.

1824. A Class started at Watchet with 16 members.

1824. First Chapel built at Watchet. Services held previously in Mr. J. Date's Loft.

1825. Sunday School commenced at Watchet.

1825. Services commenced at Porlock.

1825. Class formed at Alcombe.

1826. Class formed at Linton, Old Cleeve, and Services held at Mr. Hill's House.

1826. Chapel built at Washford (on present site).

1828. Chapel built at Wiveliscombe.

1832. New Chapel built at Dunster.

1835. Methodist Services started at Winsford.

1837. Chapel built at Porlock.

1838. Chapel built at Exford.

1839. Chapel built at Cutcombe.

1839. Centenary Celebration at Washford.

1840. Methodism started at Lynton.

1848. Chapel built at Bridgtown.

1848. Present Chapel at Wiveliscombe built.

1850. Chapel built at Alcombe.

1869. Dunster Circuit divided, and Williton became the head of a separate Circuit.

1872. Present Chapel at Watchet built.

1874. Methodist Services commenced at Capton, in Mr. Gliddon's House.

1874. Present Chapel at Minehead built.

1883. Present Chapel, Schoolroom, and Manse at Williton built.

1888. New Chapel Built at Winsford.

1893. Present Chapel at Cutcombe built.

1897. Iron Chapel erected at Monksilver.

CHAPTER THREE

Orchard Wyndham

The Wyndham Estate was fully established by the 16th century and from the 1500s onwards there were few areas in the parish that did not at one time or another come under its ownership. The house known as Orchard Wyndham is now the Wyndham family home, although this has not always been exclusively the case (see *The Book of Silverton*, Chapter 4). The summarised story of Orchard Wyndham is based on information largely extracted from the *Victoria County History* and readers are referred to that volume for further information. An estate belonging to the Orchards can be traced back to 1287 when it was owned by Thomas Orchard. It descended by marriage to the Sydenhams and thence to the Wyndhams, the succession from that time being as follows:

Orchard Wyndham, late 1800s.
(Courtesy James Date Archive)

Sir John Wyndham 1529–74
Sir John Wyndham (grandson) 1581–1645
John Wyndham (second son) 1645–49
Sir William Wyndham (created a Baronet in 1661) 1649–83
Sir Edward Wyndham 1683–95
Sir William Wyndham 1695–1740
Charles Wyndham (2nd Earl of Egremont) 1740–63
George Wyndham (3rd Earl of Egremont) 1763–37
George Francis Wyndham (4th Earl of Egremont) 1837–45
Countess of Egremont (no heir to title) 1845–76
William Wyndham of Wilts (senr) 1876–91
William Wyndham of Wilts (junr) 1891–1950
George Wyndham 1950–82
Widow and descendants of George Wyndham

In days long gone by it would seem that Orchard Wyndham was very much the 'house in the park', but with the passage of time its surrounds have changed so that it now sits in pastures and pleasant gardens. Wyndham Estate Lodge is now the estate office.

The original medieval section of the main house was an open-hall building with two cruck roofs, and smoke-blackened timbers can still be seen today. Additions were made from the 15th to the 19th centuries, and the house and outbuildings cover a large area.

From time to time special arrangements are made so that members of the public have the opportunity to see at least some of this historic building. One memorable open event at the house was on the Queen's Silver Jubilee in 1977 when a brief guide to the village was included in the celebratory programme of events. The entry on Orchard Wyndham included a macabre story about the second Sir John Wyndham's wife, Florence, who, it was related:

> *... had the misfortune to be buried at St Decuman's whilst still alive... the Sexton, either consumed with curiosity or avarice for the jewels buried with the corpse, opened the coffin to be greeted by the corpse coming out of a coma!*

To conclude the story; the sexton fled, never to be seen again. Florence herself recovered from her ordeal and year later gave birth to a son, and later still bore twins!

Top and above: *From a collection of photographs of Orchard Wyndham by James Date.* (Courtesy James Date Archive)

Right: *Wyndham memorial in St Decuman's Church.*

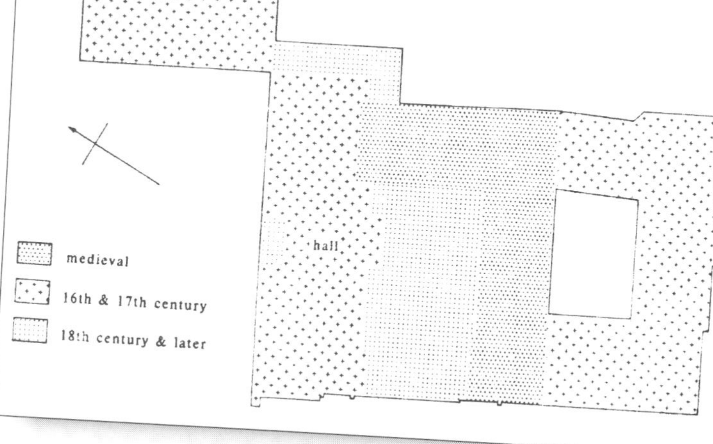

Above: *Looking up the road towards the Estate Lodge in the snow. This photograph, which hails from the Hole studios, was taken on 29 January 1937.*

Right: *Plan of the house and its additions.*

Below: *Smoke-blackened roof timbers from the cruck roof.*

Right: *The Estate Lodge, now the Estate Office.* (Courtesy James Date Archive)

Croftways before it was devastated by fire in the 1930s.

Crowds gather outside the house after the blaze.

CHAPTER FOUR

Places of Interest & Local Services

LONG STREET & 'THE REC.'

The Memorial Recreation Ground, to give it its full name, is a memorial to the men of Williton who gave their lives during the two world wars. It was purchased by Mr W. Wyndham at a time when it was divided by hedges into three fields. These were removed by ex-servicemen in 1921, the year in which the now 'Royal' British Legion was formed, and the Legion memorial to those killed during the First World War was dedicated on 9 July 1932.

The deeds to the Recreation Ground, dated 14 September 1920, contain a particularly interesting condition of sale (to Wm Wyndham Esquire) which reads as follows:

No person or persons or body of persons otherwise eligible shall be denied the privileges and use of the Trust on account of his, her or their religious or political opinions and in the management and control of the Trust premises no difference shall be made in favour of or against any person or persons or body of persons on account of their religious or political opinions...

Next to the Long Street entrance to the Recreation Ground is a house called Croftways (*opposite*). The word croft indicates a former smallholding and indeed there are a number of other crofts in the area, including North Croft, Whitecroft, Hartnells Croft and Croft House. Also recorded, though no longer in existence, are Potters Croft and Opyes Croft.

Further down the street in the same photograph stands Honeysuckle Cottage, end on to the road, which bears the date 1607 and was probably one of the main farmhouses in this part of the village.

Gymkhana at the Memorial Recreation Ground in the 1940s.

Top: *Long Street, early 1900s.*

Above: *Another view of Long Street, early 1900s.*

Left: *An early postcard of North Street.*

Above: *Lily Morle used to live in the house on the right of the road furthest from the camera. Bob Long worked at Bridge Farm and had three sons. The middle brother, Maurice, became a police inspector, and another brother, Bob, delivered milk on a bicycle.*

Left: *A view of Bridge Street before St Peter's School was built. Locals remember Miss Date, by then quite an old lady, living in the cottage on the left.*

Right: *The drive up to Orchard Wyndham which begins in Bridge Street but ends here at Lower Stream. At Stream in the 1920s there was a popular school to which children walked from Williton to attend.*

Left: *A view of Williton from Tower Hill before a great deal of development had taken place. This view looking to the north is thought to date from the 1920s.*

Right: *This photograph is thought to have been taken a little later from a lower view-point, providing a more general view looking in an easterly direction.*

Left: *Tower Hill after some early housing development.*

Right: *All hands to the harvest in a field below Larviscombe. Here the generations come together to make the last cut of the 1936 season. Tower Hill is to the south.*

Right: *The slipway at Doniford (which falls within the parish), long since gone.*

Left: *Doniford beach, 1920s. The Donkey House on the cliff has long gone. (See also* The Book of Watchet.*)*

Doniford lime kiln. Now gone, the kiln was one of many situated along the coast. Limestone was hauled from the beach by donkeys and used by builders for mortar and for decorating walls (limewash). (See also The Book of Watchet.*)*

An early postcard of the Workhouse from the front.

An early postcard of the Workhouse looking up Long Street.

THE WORKHOUSE

The 1832 Reform Act was perhaps the greatest instrument of social change in the first half of the 20th century, and the following Poor Law Amendment Act of 1834 had considerable and noticeable effect. Under the Act, Poor Law Commissioners were appointed to supervise 'Boards of Guardians', whose duty it was to administer the law. A grouping of parishes into 'Unions' led to the Williton Poor Law Union and the construction of the Workhouse in 1837/8 at a cost of £6000. Designed by Sir Gilbert Scott, it continued to serve under various names until 1948 when, under the National Assistance Act, it became a hospital.

It is thought that at one time the building housed 300 unfortunate people, mostly for short periods of time. It was a requirement that work be carried out by inmates and cracking stone for road making was a common task. Workhouse children attended the local school and were able to progress but the imbeciles tended to spend their lives in the Workhouse. By today's standards the Workhouse would have been a very hard place, but it was administered by the Williton Board of Guardians and represented one of the early efforts towards caring for the less fortunate who spent their time wandering and sleeping in the open. In the early 1900s it was commonplace for a tramp to arrive at the Williton Workhouse seeking food and water after walking from the next establishment (at Dulverton) and, having received succour, to go on his weary way once again.

Long-serving Master and Matron at the Workhouse were Mr and Mrs Baker. Their service from 1901 to 1937 was under the Board of Guardians until March 1930 (when they were stood down), then under a successor committee appointed by Somerset County Council (the elected Local Government authority from 1894). With the passing of the National Assistance Act in 1948 the building became an old people's hospital, and so continued until 1989 when it was replaced by a new, purpose-designed hospital on the Williton to Watchet road. It is hoped that the Workhouse or its site will be put to good use in the new millennium.

Above: *The Workhouse as Williton Hospital, 1980s.*
Main: *Members and officers of the Board of Guardians, 1930.*

Left: *Left to right: Frank Morgan, Dr C.F.R. Killick, Mr Stocks, Mrs Bridgwater.*

Below: *Dr Carey at the hospital together with representatives who attended the ceremony performed on the dedication of the hospital chapel.*

Below left: *Miss Leversha (seated), a member of the Brabazon Society, was guest of honour at a formal ceremony in the Brabazon Room of the hospital.*

Above: *One of the early efforts of the League of Friends was the presentation of the first colour television set at the old hospital in time for Christmas.*

Right: *Mr Morgan making his address to the gathering with Mr Tom King, MP, in the background, Open Day, 1983.*

WILLITON HOSPITAL & THE LEAGUE OF FRIENDS

The inaugural meeting of the League of Friends was held in the Rural District Council chamber on 8 April 1970 when the 100 people present elected the first committee of 15 members, with the late Mr F. Risdon as Chairman and Mr F. Morgan as his Deputy. Before the election the meeting had been addressed by Mr Dodd of the National League who gave an explanation of the objects of the League, his helpful guidance being appreciated by all concerned. Prior to the establishment of the League of Friends, the Brabazon Society had done much to help and support Williton Workhouse and the hospital, and it was the first to give financial support to the League by means of a cheque for £167.

Open days were enjoyed at the hospital and these were attended by distinguished guests of the League. It was on the occasion in 1983 that Mr Morgan made an appeal for a new hospital in the presence of the Right Hon. Tom King, MP, who joined in the spirit of the open day by conducting Watchet Town Band.

The move into a new hospital in 1988 was a great occasion for all concerned and the completion of the conservatory (named the Brabazon Room) was to the particular delight of the League which had undertaken this project at a cost of £44 000. Another project undertaken was the provision of a chapel within the hospital, the dedication of which was performed by the Bishop of Bath and Wells, Dr George Carey, now Archbishop of Canterbury.

The League continues to provide comfort and amenity at the hospital which has extended its services to a wider section of the community, and appreciates the considerable support it receives from the public. The Deputy Chairman of the first committee elected in 1970 took over the chairmanship later in that same year and Mr Frank Morgan, MBE, still serves in that capacity. The *West Somerset Free Press* reported a special reception to celebrate Frank's award of the MBE and the report on 17 May 1996 included a photograph of Frank with Mrs Bridgwater, Mr Stocks and Dr Killick in the Brabazon Room at the hospital. Dr Killick was a most respected person who made a considerable contribution to the community and, as recorded elsewhere, a road in Williton bears the family name. His association with the Workhouse, old hospital and new hospital was ongoing and he saw considerable social change during his 100 years. It is perhaps fitting to record a kindly and special relationship between the doctor and the unfortunate Joey (old Joe) who lived in the 'Big House' throughout most of his life extending from the age of 6 to 79. An ill-treated Joey was admitted to the Workhouse as an imbecile and spent the rest of his life in the same building (later known as a public assistance institution and, in 1948, as a hospital). Dr Killick kept a watchful eye on him for many years until Joe died in 1958.

Williton Hospital.

Killick Way

The library building stands near the Council Offices alongside the road known as Killick Way. At the end of Killick Way we find the purpose-designed surgery with its own car park which adjoins the west side of the Recreation Ground. Central car parks alongside Killick Way serve the central shopping area. The present Registrar's Office is in the premises adjoining Killick Way which were built to house a transformer and sales office when electricity arrived in Williton during 1929.

Top: *Fred Killick cutting the cake at an unknown celebration in the village.*

Above: *The library, erected on the site previously occupied by the fire station.*

Right: *The present-day surgery in Robert Street at the end of Killick Way.*

FIRE STATIONS

The site of the new purpose-designed fire station is approximately 100 yards from the location of a fire station that existed in the early 1900s. Here the small double-doored garage-like building still stands (*right*). The fire appliance around the turn of the century was an old horse-drawn, hand-pumped Merryweather and in the event of fire the crew were summoned by whistle, while the horses were caught and harnessed. The equipment was old and the procedure time consuming which seems to have given credence to the saying 'Keep the fire going until the fire engine arrives' and 'let 'un burn up a bit so that we can see what we're about!'

The old Fire Brigade was disbanded and the equipment scrapped in 1938 and it seems likely that this action was taken because of the Fire Brigades Act of the same year which required local authorities to ensure provision of an effective and efficient fire service. Williton RDC then had a fire station built near the Council offices, equipped it with a new engine and pump and a new brigade was formed. War was then declared and services were provided under an Emergency Act. The Williton Brigade saw service at Bristol, Bath, etc. during the Blitz. The later Act of 1947 made it the responsibility of the County Council to provide the service which we enjoy today.

The fire station near the Council Offices was demolished to make way for the new purpose-designed library. The new Fire Station, in North Road, was opened on 16 January 1993.

Above: *Opening of the new station.*
Left to right: D.W. Sully, P. Young, N. Musselwhite (HMI), Mr D.J. Huxtable (Public Protection Committee).

Top: *Fire Brigade, c.1963. Left to right, back: R. Besley, F. Berniaz, K. Bulpin, G. Turner, V. Buller, H. Gunning, R. Binding, Station Officer C. Lyddon, C. Tarr, C. Shopland, W. Symons, D. Langdon; front: F. Western, J. Smith, D. Sully, B. Cheek, P. Williams, J. Dray.*

Top: *A very early picture of the Police Station with the gas lamp outside.*

Above: *The Police Station as it is today. Little appears to have changed, although there is considerably less greenery.*

Left: *A village bobby outside the station before the Second World War, during which the inscription above the doorway of the building was removed as it would have informed any infiltrating enemies that they were in Williton.*

Police Station

The *Directory and Gazetteer* published by Morris and Co. in 1872 records that Superintendent Meare was in charge of the County Constabulary Station at Williton, which confirms that the village was then, as some would argue it is still, a suitable centre from which to provide a police service for West Somerset.

The imposing building in Bank Street was built as the Police Station with cells and living accommodation and also had a court room which was used for monthly Petty Sessions and for several years also for Parish Council meetings.

Prompted by the threat of invasion during the Second World War, orders were issued to remove signposts and place names in order to confuse and delay any enemies that might appear. When it was pointed out to the police sergeant enforcing this order that Williton was carved above the door in stone he arranged for the local mason to chisel it away. The lack of signs confused friends as well as foe and an American Army sergeant enquiring the way was most upset when a local told him that he was in fact in Egypt!

Above: *It appears that at some time this thatched cottage in Long Street was used as a toll-house. The building was re-roofed during the 1930s and the end section to the west was used as the Estate Office for the Wyndham Estate. A yard that used to exist to the rear of the building was also used for estate work.*

Left: *The toll-house at Five Bells, which was demolished in the 1950s*

Above: *Toll-house in Bridge Street.*

Tithe Map, 1840.
of WILLITON

Chapter Five

Agriculture

We live in an area surrounded by great beauty but, in fact, much of that beauty is the result of hundreds of years of farming. Under the feudal system the Crown owned all of the land which, in 1086, was recorded for William the Conqueror in the Domesday Book. Tenants in Chief were given land in exchange for service and in turn parcels of land were given to barons, knights and farmers, with serfs providing the labour. All owed first allegiance to the King and it was required that farmers gave military service as foot soldiers to the knights.

References from 1288 onwards indicate that an open-field system of farming was in operation in Williton. The open fields are thought to have belonged to a group of crofts, with a number divided into strips. It may be that these groups formed the 17 areas for tithe collection. It is also interesting to note that the strip fields are clearly discernible on the Tithe Map shown opposite.

A network of streams served to water the land of the parish and in the 15th century some streams were diverted by man-made channels called waterleats to form areas of water meadows. In addition to the leats, water was diverted from below Orchard Mill under Mamsey Bridge into Mamsey Course and Outmoor, with this flow being controlled up until the present day, as are the north and north-east outflows.

The small arable units of land produced wheat, oats, beans and peas, but by the end of the 17th century Parsonage Farm (probably the largest at that time) also had a flock of sheep, pigs, bullocks and horses. Prior to this the proportion of arable to grassland had been approximately two to one, but eventually when the number of farming units was reduced the balance evened out (by the end of the 19th century there were 12 principal farming units).

By the 17th century the Wyndham Estate had become the major landowner, but tenant farmers continued to farm the land. Agricultural fairs were established in 1767 (mainly for the sale of hardware) and these continued for about 100 years. From 1860 cattle markets were held in April and December and these were supplemented by a summer fair/market. Later, in 1866, an additional market was established for pigs and sheep and this or a similar pattern of markets was followed until the advent of the Second World War. The market site was subsequently occupied by Gliddon & Sons, Agricultural Engineers.

The earliest wooden single-furrow ploughs, drawn first by man and then beasts, were, it would seem, hewn from small trees with the aid of axe and adze, but with the use of improved iron tools, followed by iron implements, the working of the land to greater effect soon followed. The demands on the farmworkers became more varied, as did those on the services of shoesmiths and blacksmiths. More horses were being worked in the fields and iron implements and tools were widely introduced. The splendid Shire horses were the pride and joy of their owners and they performed their work well, but the breed was gradually superseded by machine and the blacksmith to some extent was replaced by the agricultural engineer.

The steam engine was introduced into farmyards to drive pulley shafts which in turn would drive such machinery as was required. In time the steam engine was replaced by diesel engines and electric motors. With facilities available in the farmyard it was desirable to haul the produce of the fields to the farm building for processing or storage and the traditional horse and cart was replaced by the tractor and trailer. Modern demands on our farmers are such that many have to attempt to produce crops on land which in their better judgement would not be used for that purpose, but survival demands that they must.

Prior to the Second World War, rotation of crops was the norm and the ground was fertilised with animal manure but shortage of food demanded that extreme measures be taken to feed the nation. Chemicals were used to increase crops by early re-use of land and this practice has continued to this day. Subsidies are paid, but competition has resulted in payments for produce falling to levels which do not properly reward the farmer. Now, the growing trend is towards labour-intensive, but perhaps in the long term, more rewarding organics.

Harvest

Above: *Harvest scene at Williton just after the Second World War. On top of thresher, left to right: D. Langdon, F. Pugsley ('Yorkie'); on the ground: H. Hill, E. Chilcott, A. Jones, T. Nethercott, Ralph Sutton (with cider jar), F. Bulpin ('Boxhat'), two Land Army girls, ?, H. Nethercott.*

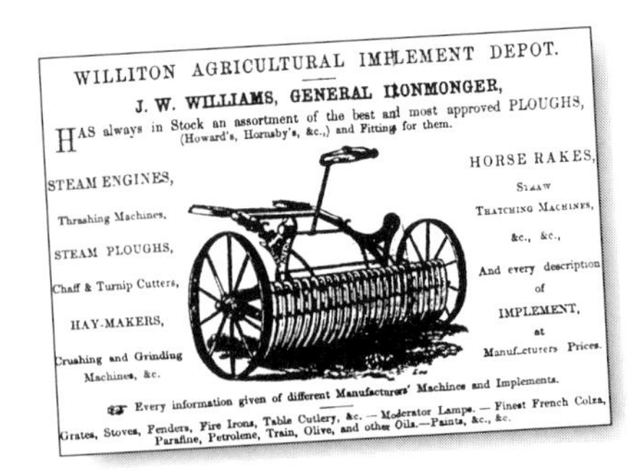

Above, centre and right: *Threshing corn in the age of steam.*

Williton Market

Battered but rather lovely, these two old photographs show Williton Market on the ground and surrounds of the area now occupied by Gliddons, c.1900.

Kebby's Farm, which stood near the entrance to the present Littlebrook Estate, the main building fronting Long Street. The last farmer here was Bill Moorman.

The farm at nearby Stream, part of the Wyndham Estate.

Wibble Farm, which is now a nursery.

Bridge Farm.

Left: *Harry Kerslake at the Half Acre Forge.*

Below: *Harry Kerslake at the Robert Street Forge.*

Below left: *A gold medal award for shoeing presented to Harry Kerslake.*

Left: *Thomas Kerslake at Washford Forge.*

Below left: *A Kerslake lorry at Half Acre. The haulier's business was developed by Arthur Kerslake.*

Below right: *Arthur Kerslake and the horse Noble at Half Acre in 1924. Visible in the left foreground is the corner of the table which was used to fit cartwheel rims.*

The Kerslakes

Life for many in rural areas in the early-19th century was not so much a matter of striving for a certain quality of life as one of survival. Such work as was available other than in agriculture tended to be limited to the small number who were fortunate enough to be apprenticed or articled to a craftsman or agent of some kind. Living at Halberton, near Tiverton, was James Kerslake, who had served an apprenticeship as a blacksmith and progressed to the position of journeyman blacksmith; with confidence in his skill he decided to make his way as his own master. It is said that in 1864 James set out walking from Halberton to establish himself in business; having walked to Raleigh's Cross he spun a coin to decide which route to follow and the result was the establishment of his business at The Forge in Half Acre at Williton. This early photograph is of James with his wife Ellen.

Above: *Left to right: E. Chilcott, apprentice, ?, Harry Kerslake, James Kerslake and granddaughter at Vellow Forge.*

Left: *The Kerslake family, c.1930.*

The traditional country method of cider making in the early 1950s practised by, left to right: C. Bulpin, C. Tremlett, H. ('Major') Langdon, E. Chilcott, S. Barker, C. Capel, G. Hall and Mr Fermor.

Members of the Women's Land Army outside their hostel at The Limes, Long Street, during the 1940s.

GLIDDONS

For well over a century and a half the name Gliddon has been synonymous with agriculture and engineering, the family having built up a fine trade which now stretches across Somerset to Cornwall from its base at Williton. John Gliddon was in business at Barnstaple in 1833 when he met his wife, and decided to sell up and move to Williton.

The business of John Gliddon in Bank Street prospered, he had three sons – John Wesley, Benjamin and Henry – and was able to furnish them with a good education. During his schooling, John (senr) branched out and started selling ploughs and washing equipment, and manufacturing kitchen ranges. Benjamin served an apprenticeship with H. Beare & Sons at Newton Abbot and then returned to the family business to join Henry, who was helping his father. John Wesley, meanwhile, was away fighting in the Crimean War and although he returned and began to help in the family business, he was to die young, a year before his father, in 1880. On the death of John (senr) one year later, Benjamin took over and was assisted by Henry.

Benjamin's son Arthur served an apprenticeship with engine makers Richard Hornsby & Sons, of Grantham, and brought his new-found experience to the business which was then expanded to include horse-drawn farm implements and later motorised farm equipment, tractors and cars. The heavy engineering part of the company was carried out over the hill at Gliddon's Foundry in Watchet which operated until 1948 (see *The Book of Watchet*). Farriers provided a service from the Gliddons' High Street premises in Williton which, in time, became a garage.

Arthur Gliddon's sons John and Laity saw the firm into the tractor age and the association with Ferguson's hydraulically-equipped machine. David and Ben Gliddon, sons of John and Laity respectively, are now at the helm of the business which has served Williton long and well. Many residents of the village have been employed in the business and have contributed to its success.

In the long history of the *Free Press* it is doubtful whether there has ever been such a crisis week as that in the late 1940s which culminated with the appearance of a tractor in the press rooms! The printers at the *Free Press* office in Williton were having trouble with the old gas engine which powered the machinery and which, with its huge wheel, served as the heartbeat of the works. It finally seized up and was kicked, cursed and subjected to every known form of the kiss of life. Even some powerful explicit adjectives from Harry Burge were of no avail! Its day was done, and it looked as though for the first time in its history there would be no publication of the paper that week. It was then that an apparently ridiculous plan was born out of the crisis. Laughable it might have been but in fact it worked and the credit was due to the late Mr A.L. Gliddon, of Messrs J. Gliddon & Sons. A farm tractor was brought into the building and jacked up. It roared into action and with a Heath Robinson system of belts, shafts and wheels, a connection was made that turned the main printing press. The sight of the papers flopping into the delivery tray had the printers drinking a toast to agriculture! The 'phut-phut-pop-phut' of that old gas engine as it fired into life had been an early-morning call for North Street residents for years, and many were glad to see its demise. As also must have been Harry Burge, who used to go down to the works at 5.30a.m. to fire up the gas engine ready for when the printers went into work at 6a.m.

In this cartoon by Kwinty, Gliddon's greasers come to the rescue of the Free Press *printers.*

Gliddons' premises in Williton. Frank Stevens was the manager of the garage in the top picture in early times and Howard Gunning also worked there. Toby Sully lived in the cottage in the centre of the picture which was demolished to make way for the petrol pumps. John Gliddon came from Barnstaple to open the hardware shop in the above picture in 1833. The shop on the right was a pharmacy, a sweet shop, then a furniture shop. Further north was a men's outfitters. All were run by Hedley and Claude Hann, their business being founded by their father Theodore William Hann.

Gliddons employees gather for the retirement party of Harry Routley and George Salter in 1966. Included are: Derek Lile, Michael Agg, 'Jack' Arthur Bellamy, Fred Smith, Jeremy Massey Crosse, D. Tremlett, Dick Mathews, Cyril Newbert, David Mortimer, Heather Bryant, Colin Chilcott, M. Hendy, Rob Johnson, Alan Vigars, Bryan Slader, Jock Parsons, Jimmy Wheeler, David (Fred) Lee, Richard Melhuish, Desmond Hoare, George Turner, Derek Matravers, Frank Garside, Jim Steer, J.G., Reg Hendy, Trevor Nethercott, David Burge, Bill Symons, Ray Coles, Ben Gliddon, David Gliddon, Frank Cattle, Barry Suchley, George Salter. John Gliddon presented gold watches to George Salter and Harry Routley, both of whom worked for Gliddons for 50 years. In the picture are two others, younger then, Derek Lile and Cyril Newbert, who both went on to complete 50 years for the firm.

Gliddons football team, 1932.
Left to right, back: George Salter, John Gliddon, Roy Davis, A. Laity Gliddon, Ronald S. Gliddon; seated: ?, E. Blackwell, Toby Sully, ?, Maurice Tiller; on ground: Howard Gunning.

The wedding of Arthur Stoate to Mabel Gliddon. Left to right, standing: Leonard Stoate, ?, Arthur Stoate, Mabel Gliddon, Ben Gliddon; sitting: James Stoate (of Torre), Anna Gliddon.

A family gathering in the garden behind the ironmongers shop in Priest Street.
Left to right, standing: Ethel, John, ?; seated: Arthur, Anna, Ben, Harry Beare; on ground: Mabel, Linda.

Above: *A.H. Gliddon surveys a Bean (or perhaps a Singer) car in the early 1920s. It is not known whether the vehicle was his own or a customer's.*

Right: *A.H. Gliddon with part of a steam engine which he made while an apprentice at Ruston & Hornsby in Grantham. In those days one had to pay to become an apprentice!*

Above: *Laity and John Gliddon on a tandem.*

Right: *Ben Gliddon cycling in Long Street. He is reputed to have carried castings from the Watchet foundry back to Williton on his bicycle.*

The Jones and Martin families. The old gentleman in the centre is Charlie Jones of J. Jones & Son. Edward Martin's father, the late Charlie Martin (with open-neck shirt, 2nd from right), was brought up by Charlie and Lilian Jones and took over the family business.

Charlie, Edward and Andrew Martin, c.1997.

Chapter Six

Williton Businesses

Williton's 1872 entry in *Morris & Co. Commercial Directory and Gazetteer* included the following:

Name	Business	Location
J. Sparks	*Joiner*	*Long St.*
H. Holcombe	*Stationmaster*	*Long St.*
H. White	*Solicitor*	*Long St.*
T. Kent	*Shopkeeper*	*Long St.*
H.H. Hole	*Photographer*	*Long St.*
T. Fisher	*Horse Dealer*	*Long St.*
J. Blackman	*Schoolmaster*	*Long St.*
Mrs S. Brice	*Baker*	*Long St.*
Thomas Fry [Landlord]	*Railway Hotel*	*Long St.*
T. Hawkes	*Land Agent*	*Long St.*
T. Casson	*Saddle Maker*	*Long St.*
J.H. Reynett	*Surgeon*	*Long St.*
A. Barber	*Weslyan Reverend*	*Long St.*
Mrs Tuttiett	*Doctor's Widow*	*Long St.*
T. Horne	*Surveyor*	*Long St.*
T. Langdon	*Gentleman*	*Long St.*
William Collins	*Gentleman*	*Long St.*
J. Collins	*Steward*	*Long St.*
E. Penny	*Revenue Officer*	*Long St.*
Walter Frost	*Surgeon*	*Long St.*
Ann Fowler	*Milliner*	*Long St.*
Miss Churchills	*Milliner*	*Long St.*
W. Bond	*Veterinary Surgeon*	*Long St.*
John Dore [Landlord]	*New Inn*	*Long St.*
Joseph Forster Foot [Master]	*Union Workhouse*	*Long St.*
W.H. White [Hon. Sec.]	*Reading Rooms*	*Long St.*
J. Jones [Gardener/Nurseryman]	*Nursery*	*Long St.*
Mrs E. Smith [Laundress]	*Laundry*	*Long St.*
W. Jones [Plumber]	*Tradesman*	*Long St.*
Sparks [Bros]	*Organ Builders*	*Long St.*
T. Langdon	*Grocer*	*Long St.*
A. Hurley	*Miller*	*Orchard Mill*
William Meare	*Constab. Station*	*Priest St.*
S. Dunn [Landlord]	*Egremont Hotel*	*Priest St.*
J. Gliddon	*Ironmonger*	*Priest St.*
J. Rossiter	*Gardener*	*Priest St.*
S. Cox [West Somerset Free Press]		*Shutgate St.*
J. Sitson	*Evangelist*	*Shutgate St.*
W. Stevens	*Dairyman*	*Shutgate St.*
Miss E. Torrington		*Shutgate St.*
R. Trebble	*Butcher*	*Shutgate St.*
J. Trebble	*Tailor*	*Shutgate St.*
P. Williams	*Wheelwright*	*Shutgate St.*
J. and W. Sparks		*Shutgate St.*
W. Besley	*Mason*	*Shutgate St.*
S. Scott [Landlord]	*Mason's Arms*	*Shutgate St.*
Mrs S. Cole	*Fishmonger*	*Bob Lane*
R. Pippen	*Fishmonger*	*Bob Lane*
T. Hurley	*Gardener*	*Bob Lane*
T. Cridland	*Bootmaker and Seedsman*	*Bob Lane*
J.W. Williams	*Grocer etc*	*Bob Lane*
J. Elliott	*Carrier*	*Bob Lane*
T. Rice	*Baker*	*Bob Lane*
F. Burton	*Bootmaker*	*Bridge St.*
P. Hutchings	*Butcher*	*Bridge St.*
M. Langdon	*Butcher*	*Bridge St.*
Geo Hake [Postmaster]	*Post Office and Telegraph Office*	*Fore St.*
John Walter Williams [Agent]	*Quantock Savings Bank*	*Fore St.*
J. Langdon	*Joiner*	*Fore St.*
G. Eames	*Bootmaker*	*Fore St.*
J. Fry	*Coppersmith*	*Fore St.*
J. Hake	*Draper*	*Fore St.*
Strong & Co.	*Grocers, etc.*	*Fore St.*
H. Churchill	*Saddlers*	*Half Acre*
G. Howe	*Shopkeeper*	*Half Acre*
W. Langdon	*Bootmaker*	*Half Acre*
G. Trebble	*Shoemaker*	*Half Acre*
A. Dore	*Farm Bailiff*	*Half Acre*
Mrs A. M. Williams	*Catwell Cottage*	*Half Acre*
J. Pursey	*Catwell House/ Farmer*	*Half Acre*
J. Thristle	*Watchmaker*	*High St.*
J. Sully	*Hairdresser*	*High St.*
Mrs F. Greenslade	*Tallow Chandler*	*High St.*
J. Chibbett	*Builder*	*High St.*
H. Sparks [Landlord]	*Wyndham Arms*	*High St.*
G. Westcott	*Blacksmith*	*High St.*
J. Ward	*Shopkeeper*	*High St.*
Charles Saunders Esq. [Judge]	*County Court*	
Edwin Perry [Officer]	*Inland Revenue Office*	
	Stuckey's Bank	
T. Hosegood	*Farmer*	
George Hole	*Carpenter*	
H. Routley	*Tailor*	
Revd Heathcote	*Incumbent*	*Eastfield*

LOT 48.

(COLOURED RED ON PLAN).

ALL THAT

Stone-built and Slated Dwelling-house and Saddler's Shop,

At Corner of High Street and Half Acre, in the occupation of Mr. W. W. CHURCHILL, on a yearly Michaelmas tenancy, at the Annual Rent of £17, containing Tiled Entrance Lobby, 9 Bed and Sitting-rooms, Kitchen, and Offices; Front Shop and Workshop at back, with Loft over; at back is Yard, with Entrance from High Street, with Lean-to Wash-house and Store Sheds; small Garden.

Water supplied by Pump, also Town Water laid on.

This Lot is sold subject to the right of Lot 12 to Light for 2 Windows overlooking this Lot, and also subject to the right of Lot 12 to drain the W.C., &c., on such Lot into the drains upon this Lot, and also subject to the right of the Owner and Occupiers of Lot 47 to drain the Roof Water on to this Lot.

Top: *H.H. Hole postcard of Long Street looking eastwards, the road as yet unmade. The little girls in Edwardian dress are standing in front of 'the little house'. Next door is No.25 with its shop.*

Centre: *The same view around 30 years later with a child outside the sweet shop, c.1930s. Nearby is the large window of the furniture shop. Across the road was Hole's photographic studio (now the dentist's) where at one time, after the closure of the sweet shop, sweets could also be bought.*

Above: *Sales description for the premises (Lot 48) from the Wyndham Estate Sale, 1919.*

Long Street Businesses

Left: *The building occupied by Mr E.G. Ashman's electrical business in this photograph was that previously occupied by Mr Casson (saddler). Before it was returned to use as a private residence it was in turn occupied as a radio and TV shop (Minehead Radio), car-accessory shop and a material and gift shop. Here Ted Ashman is standing with his van outside his electrical shop after a heavy fall of snow.*

Right: *In about 1905 a tailor's shop existed on the premises that were used as a library in Long Street prior to the opening of the new facility in Killick Way. This building has now been added to the adjoining private house. Numerous other small businesses were conducted in Long Street, some of which were run from cottages, and the sign of Mr Buncombe (blacksmith) could be seen on the wall of one of the cottages with a walkway raised above the level of the old water-course that ran down the street. The blacksmith's workshop itself was in Robert Street. Records of smithies can also be found on sites now occupied by Gliddons Garage, the Pottery and at a site set back from the road in North Street. The blacksmith's sign of Mr Buncombe can just be seen in the background of this snowy scene from 1922 showing Hibbert's milkman from Watchet tackling the slippery roads.*

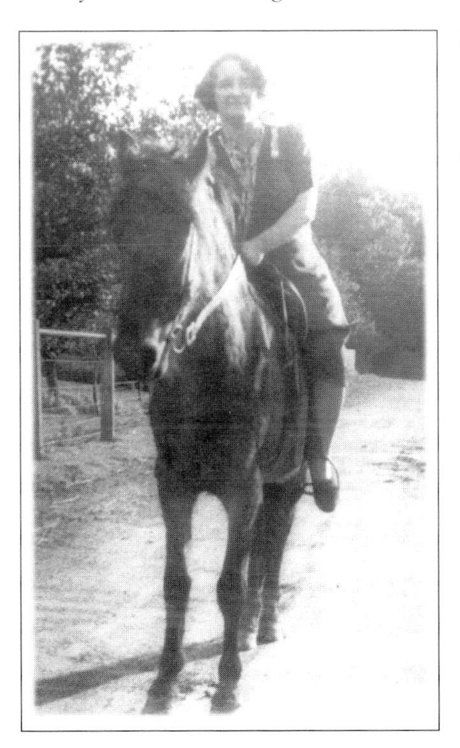

Above and left: *C.1900 a bakery business was run from premises opposite the Railway Hotel/Foresters Arms, and later a guest house and café were run there by a Mr and Mrs Wilcox. Mrs Wilcox was very fond of animals and is seen here, c.1950, on horseback and with the ducks and fowls in the yard behind the café. The premises were eventually replaced by bungalows.*

Some of the printing and many of the photographs relating to Williton and district can be attributed to the Hole family, whose business began in 1856. Many of the photographs in this volume are undoubtedly the work of the Holes, although not all of them can be identified as such.

Top and below: *The Hole family business premises.*

Above: *H.H. Hole's photographs covered a multitude of subjects. This lovely shot of St Peter's Church is typical of the general views which the firm produced of Williton.*

Left and below: *Invariably H.H. Hole would be present at any significant local event to record it for posterity. The photograph on the left shows MP Croom-Johnson at Williton, 31 May 1919. The image below strikes a lighter chord, portraying a well-supported local sporting event, the marathon run all the way to Porlock and back – here pictured in 1909 as the runners gather before the start at Williton.*

Left: *The Hole family business was not limited to the immediate vicinity of Williton. Postcards survive originating in the Hole studio which cover an area stretching throughout a substantial portion of West Somerset as this rare image of miners at the top of the Mineral Line demonstrates.*

Right: *Another wonderfully evocative image from the Hole studio of West Adit, Colton Pit at the Brendon Hill Mines.*

Jones Bakery business was started in 1877 by Mr W.H. Jones, who was later joined by his sons Charles and Sam. This postcard shows the shop as it was in the early years of the business when bread was delivered by horse and cart driven by Charles and Sam. The business was taken over by the late Norman Jones, son of Sam, and was sold on Norman's retirement but continues to trade under the same name.

Jones Bakery, 1930s, and an advertisement for the shop from a guide to Somerset of 1970.

Top and above: *J. Chibbett & Sons, builders. It seems likely that at one time J. Chibbett & Sons were the largest employers in Williton. The then thatched premises in the High Street served as their base and the firm had its own football team, pictured here. Accounts show that in 1894, 25 chimneys at the Workhouse were swept for 12.6d. and a funeral was conducted at a total cost of £2.18.6d.*

Left: *Faulkener's Stores.*

Fore Street Businesses

PLEASE MAKE A MEMO. OF THIS ADDRESS:–
BREWER HOWELL,
Woollen Draper, Tailor, Hatter, and General Outfitter,
HIGH-STREET, WILLITON.

The right Address for
"A good selection of Cloths and Trimmings."

The right Address for
"Value for your Money."

The right Address for
"Good Materials, good Workmanship, and good Fit."

The right Address for
"Every Article of Gentlemen's Clothing."

The right Address for
"Prompt execution of orders."

The right Address for
"Hats and Caps of every description."

BREWER HOWELL, HIGH-STREET, WILLITON.

SECOND DELIVERY
of
HATS AND CAPS FOR THE PRESENT SEASON.
The largest Stock and best value in West Somerset, at
BREWER HOWELL'S, HIGH-STREET, WILLITON.

Above: *This Fore Street photograph of busy shoppers was taken when the roofs were still thatched, c.1920s.*

Left: *Advertisement for two High Street businesses.*

Right: *Mother Shipton's Café, c.1950s.*

Below: *The shop of Parsons and Hann.*

PARSONS & HANN Ltd.
CONTRACTORS TO H.M. WAR OFFICE AND THE BRITISH BROADCASTING CORPORATION

The Oldest Established and Most Up-to-date Shopping Centre of the West Country

Weekly Deliveries throughout the district by our own vans

If you are taking your holidays in the District, we can give you a Service that represents years of experience, and the Quality of the Goods we handle are the Finest it is possible to procure

Departments:
High Class Grocery and Provisions
Drapery & Millinery — Gent's Clothing & Outfitting
Reliable Footwear
China, Glass and Household Ironmongery
Bedding and Furnishing

CALL AT OUR PHARMACIES
WILLITON 12 and WATCHET 343

Toilet Requisites of every Description
Bring your Films to us for Developing and Printing

ALL BUSES STOP OUTSIDE OUR PREMISES

WILLITON & WASHFORD
Phone: WILLITON 12 — WASHFORD 206

Above: *The business of Mr W. Horner, grocer and draper, was established in c.1898 in the shop at the right-hand end of the site of the present-day Co-op. The dealer in the cart (c.1900) worked as, among other things, a venison supplier. A deer carcass can be seen, but it is not certain if it was being offered to Mr Horner for sale. The dealer was Mr Rich, whose prosperity depended largely on the hunt's success and his whereabouts at the time of despatch.*

Left: *At the end of the road is the cart of Jones Bakery driven by Charles or Sam.*

Below: *An early view of Fore Street.*

The premises of W.W. Churchill, the saddle and harness maker at Half Acre.

Wayside Café, Priest Street.

Above: *North Street with the gas and electric street lights still in position. Also visible is a sign board advertising accommodation from Mr and Mrs W.J.D. Venn. Mr Venn was a postman and an excellent musician. Behind these buildings in the 19th century was a carriage and wagon works run by the Williams family, who were wheelwrights by trade. On the opposite side of the road are the printing works of the* West Somerset Free Press.

Above: *The van is outside the premises which were at one time those of a bootmaker and close to the smithy entrance. Behind the smithy there was once both a builder and an upholsterer.*

Left: *North Street Carriage and Wagon Works. Proprietor, Mr P. Williams, is one of the men wearing a bowler hat.*

Above: *This is thought to be a picture of one of the Jones brothers delivering in Bridge Street. The scene of peaceful cottages belies the fact that numerous businesses have been run from Bridge Street down through the centuries, among them the butcher's shops of M. Langdon and P. Hutchings, and a bootmaker's enterprise, that of F. Burton, all of which were recorded as being in existence in 1872.*

Left: *Mr Reg Sutton at Orchard Mill, Williton. The mill continued in service until about 1967 and then operated with an overshot wheel driving two pairs of stones to grind wheat, barley, oats, maize and beans.*

Below: *A photograph of the mill from the Hole studios. The mill building now houses the Bakelite Museum.*

Goodlands Builders Merchants were established in 1930. In this photograph Mr E. Bale is standing in the yard.

An advertisement for Goodlands which was printed in the issue of the West Somerset Free Press *from Friday 26 March 1976, marking the re-opening of the West Somerset Railway.*

WILLITON, SOMERSET

In the midst of some of the most Beautiful Scenery in England and close to the famous Quantock Hills, and about a mile from the Sea at Watchet.

Highly Important Sale

— of —

VALUABLE FREEHOLD

Fully-Licensed Hotels,

KNOWN AS THE

"EGREMONT," "RAILWAY," & "WYNDHAM ARMS"; and

:-: INNS, :-:

Known as "MASONS' ARMS" and "NEW INN," and other

BUSINESS PREMISES.

Also Several Freehold and Very Comfortable Roomy Medium - sized

RESIDENCES,

With Good Gardens, and some with Paddocks attached; also Picturesque

Cottage Residences & Cottages,

Mostly with Large Gardens, which will be SOLD BY AUCTION, by

Messrs. RISDON & LEVERSHA

Instructed by W. WYNDHAM, Esq., at the

EGREMONT HOTEL, in WILLITON,

ON

Thursday, 18th December, 1919,

AT 1.30 P.M.

Subject to the Conditions of Sale printed herein, and such other Conditions as will be read at time of Sale.

The earliest known inn at Williton was almost certainly the Blue Anchor, a 16th-century alehouse situated on the site of the present Egremont Hotel. Mention can also be found of the Pelican which seems to have been established by 1686 at a location not known, also of a Red Lion Inn on the Post Office site in Fore Street (in 1736) and of the Kings Arms at North Street (Shutgate Street) in 1788. Nearby the Masons Arms has been known to exist for many years. Brief reference can also be found to a Shutgate Inn on the site of the Shutgate toll-house. The Masons Arms was a beerhouse in 1839 and was known as the Masons Arms at the time of the sale of some Wyndham Estate properties in 1919.

Lot 4.

The Fully-Licensed Premises,

"The Mason's Arms Inn,"

Above: *The Masons Arms, c.1920.*

Below: *Today the Masons Arms is the only remaining thatched licensed premises in Williton.*

Above: *The Masons Arms formed Lot 4 in the 1919 Wyndham Estate sale. According to notes by T. Hawkes in 1903, much of the inn was 'built on a leasehold site by the Besleys, father and sons, who were masons.' Mr Hawkes also noted: 'I recollect an open gutter from the Egremont Hotel towards Horners and thence to the Masons Arms. This was a dangerous gutter on dark nights and was covered about 60 or more years ago.'*

Lot 1.

(COLOURED BLUE ON PLAN).

The exceedingly valuable Fully-Licensed Family and Commercial House

KNOWN AS

"The Egremont Hotel,"

Occupying a coveted position at the Junction of Three Main Roads, in the Town of Williton, about ¼ mile from the Railway Station.

THE HOTEL

Is Stone-built, with Slate Roof, and contains Lobby leading to main Entrance Hall; Bar Entrance, large and comfortable Bar, with Tiled Register Grate, and lighted with 2 Windows; Smoking-room, Beer and Spirit Cellars, Private Sitting-room, with Register Grate; large Kitchen, with Herald Range and Sink with Cold Water Tap; Scullery, with Sink (H. and C.); large cool Dairy and Larder.

COFFEE - ROOM, with Register Grate.

DINING - ROOM, 20ft. by 18ft., with Tiled Register Grate and Fitted Cupboards.

SITTING - ROOM, 13ft. by 12ft., with Tiled Register Grate.

BILLIARD - ROOM, 23ft. 9in. by [illegible]ft. [illegible]in., with Grate and Bay Window, W.C.

ON FIRST FLOOR, approached by Principal and Secondary Staircases, are 9 GOOD BEDROOMS ([illegible] with Grates).

SITTING - ROOM, with Tiled Register Grate.

ASSEMBLY - ROOM, 48ft. 9in. by 17ft., with 2 Fireplaces, and lighted by 2 large Windows.

Bath-room, with Lavatory Basin and Hot and Cold Water Supplies, and Heated Linen Cupboard; W.C., Housemaid's Closet, and 2 Servants' Bedrooms.

ON THE SECOND FLOOR are 4 Bedrooms (2 with Fireplaces).

THE OUTBUILDINGS

Include Stone and Slated Stabling for 12 Horses, with Loft over; another Stable for 9 Horses, large Coach-house, with Loft over; Harness-room, Carriage Shed, and Garage; Beer and Mineral Water Cellars, Ash-house, and Urinal.

Stone-built and Slated Tap, comprising Tap Room, with Grate; Kitchen, Scullery, and 2 Bedrooms; W.C., Coal-house, Beer Cellar, and Brew-house.

Town Water and Gas laid on.

Large and productive Kitchen Garden, with Skittle Alley.

Let upon a Yearly Christmas Tenancy to Messrs. HANCOCK & SONS, LTD., at an apportioned yearly Rent of £40.

The Commuted Tithe Rent-charges payable are 1d. per annum.

No Land Tax.

The Egremont Hotel, with entrances in Fore Street and Bank Street, was built c.1830 and was at that time known as The Wyndham Hotel, but this building was preceded in the 16th century by an alehouse called the Blue Anchor, later becoming a quite large coaching house known as the Coach and Horses Inn, which was the centre for stagecoach activity in the second half of the 18th century. The change in name from The Wyndham Hotel to The Egremont Hotel occurred in 1842.

Top: *An unusual view of Fore Street highlighting the Egremont Hotel Tap. Note the parking area beside the hotel which is still in use today.*

Inset: *'Nobby' Boyles' party outside the Egremont Hotel Tap in the hotel cart. This building now houses an estate agency and a hairdressing salon.*

Left: *The Egremont was Lot 1 in the Wyndham Estate sale of 1919.*

Right: *The White House Hotel was formerly a large private house with enclosed frontage and a carriage-way protected by gates at each end. The house was largely rebuilt around 1850 and later became the attractive hotel we see today. Many parties and fêtes were held there in earlier years, and during the autumn boys were often to be seen nipping through the gates to pinch conkers from the horse-chestnut trees at the front of the house.*

Lot 5.

(COLOURED RED ON PLAN.)

The Fully-Licensed Premises,

"The New Inn,"

Situate in Long Street, Williton.

The Inn is Stone-built and Thatched, and contains :—Bar, Tap Room, Bar Parlour, Sitting-room with Tiled Register Grate; Kitchen, with Range; Larder, large Stone and Slated Lean-to Beer Cellar, 3 Bedrooms, and Store Room.

Outside are Range of Sheds, Stone and Tiled Cow Sheds, 3 Stalls and Loose Box, Stone and Slated Cider House, with Loft over, and Root House; Yard, with Entrance from Long Street.

The whole is let on a Yearly Michaelmas Tenancy to Messrs. WM. HANCOCK & SONS, LTD., at the annual rent of £30.

Adjoining is Stone-built and Thatched 5-roomed Dwelling-house, with Tailor's Shop; also Lean-to Stone-built and Slated Workshop and W.C., let to Mr. A. GREEN on a Weekly Tenancy, at a weekly apportioned Rent of 3s. 9d., the Landlord paying the rates.

Water and Gas laid on.

The Commuted Tithe Rent-charges are 1d. per annum.

No Land Tax.

This Lot is sold subject to the right of the Owner and Occupiers of the adjoining

Above and left: *Next door to The White House Hotel is the Royal Huntsman, in earlier days known as The New Inn and the subject of a story relating to the discovery of human remains when a mound was removed from its rear yard in or around 1850. Legend has it that in early times travellers were lured to the inn and murdered. The pub was Lot 5 in the Wyndham Estate Sale.*

The Foresters Arms Hotel was a private dwelling house thought to date from 1624. In about 1810 parts of the premises were used as a beerhouse known as The White Horse. In 1850 the entire premises were licensed as a hotel and named The Lamb Inn. With the coming of the railway in 1862 the name of the hotel was changed to The Railway Hotel, but in 1984 the name was changed again to become The Foresters Arms Hotel.

Lot 3.

COLOURED RED ON PLAN

The valuable Fully-Licensed Premises,

"The Railway Hotel,"

Situate in Long Street, Williton, close to the Railway Station

THE HOTEL

Is Stone-built, with good Slate Roof, and contains:—Two Entrances, Bar, with Fireplace; Tap-room, 2 Sitting-rooms, with Fireplaces; Bar Parlour, with Fireplace; Kitchen, with Range; Scullery, with Sink (Cold Water Tap); Dairy, Wash-house, with Furnace; Store-room, Cellar, W.C.

On First Floor approached by 3 Staircases, are 7 Bedrooms (4 with Fire-places) 2 Store-rooms and Linen Cupboard.

Town Water and Gas laid on.

THE OUTBUILDINGS

Comprise:—Brick and Slated Coach-house or Garage, about 45ft. by 18ft.; Lean-to Carriage Shed, Urinal, Wood and Iron Skittle Alley (Gas laid on), Stone and Tiled Stabling for 10 Horses, Stone and Iron Cow Shed.

Range of Wood and Slated Stabling and Cow Sheds, large Yard, small Garden.

Let upon Yearly Lady-day Tenancy to Messrs. Wm. Hancock & Sons, Ltd., at the yearly Rent of £60.

The Commuted Tithe Rent-charge is 1d. per annum.

No Land Tax.

This Lot is sold with a right to Light for 7 windows overlooking Lot 7, and also with the right to Drain the Roof Water on to Lot 7 through the stackpipe at the S.W. corner of the Hotel. The Lot is also sold with a right to receive the Town Water and to

Left: *The inn was Lot 3 in the Estate sale.*

Below: *The Foresters in the late 1990s.*

Left: *Opened in 1800, the Wyndham Arms offered an assembly room and stabling for horses. The property was sold to the brewing company Starkeys in 1919. It has recently been sold again and is once more in private hands.*

During the 1800s four banks ran in Williton: Quantock Savings Bank, Parrs Bank, Stuckeys Bank and the Wilts and Dorset Bank. It seems that the Quantock Savings Bank and the Wilts and Dorset Bank provided a service from premises on the present Co-op Stores site. Stuckeys Bank was where NatWest stands today. This building was erected c.1870 and Parrs provided a service there before merging with Stuckeys. Today services in Williton are provided by NatWest and Lloyds TSB.

Top: *The Wilts & Dorset Bank.*

Above: *An early Lloyds Bank on the County Stores site.*

Left: *A very faded photograph of Stuckeys Bank.*

The proprietors and staff of the Free Press *celebrating 125 years of the paper in 1985. Left to right, front (seated): M. Chidgey, Mrs H.J. Burge, H.J. Burge, Mrs G. Purcell, Ray Tindle (Chairman), Mrs Tindle, H.R. Dickinson (vice-Chairman), G. Purcell (editor), R. Taylor, R. Chave, K. Stockwell. Others include: Mrs N. Sully, D. Parkman, N. Sully, P. Date, N. Mould, Miss D. Clarke, D. Milton, Mrs D. Milton, N. Humphries, Mrs J. Jones, J. Jones, R. Willis, R. Treadaway, M. Newbert, Mrs M. Newbert, G. Walton, J. McTiffin, F. Cammidge, M. Hayes, N. Ridler, K. Caswell, Mrs R. Barron, R. Barron, D.W. Sully, Mrs D.W. Sully, R. Goring, ? Toth, Mrs L. Toth, K.W. Towells, Mrs K.W. Towells, Mrs R. Goring, Mrs M. Hayes, Mrs N. Ridler, Mrs J. Caswell, Mrs K. Cammidge, Mrs P. Smith, K. Rayner, Mrs K. Rayner, Mrs S. Templeman, Mrs J. Gibbins, W. McCord, Mrs W. McCord, A.W. Sully, Mrs A.W. Sully, Mrs R. Chave, Mrs M. Chidgey, Mrs K. Stockwell, Mrs T. McGowran, T. McGowran, Mrs K. Loughnam, K. Loughnam, C. Stone, Mrs C. Stone, C. Christmas, Mrs C. Christmas, A.F. Knight, Mrs A.F. Knight.*

Chapter Seven

West Somerset Free Press

Mr Samuel Cox, who was born at Watchet, took possession in January 1848 of part of a small house in Fore Street near the present Post Office and pulled it down for the purpose of establishing a printing, bookbinding, stationery and book-selling business on the site. The next year saw Mr Cox's removal to Long Street, on the eastern side of the Royal Huntsman (then the New Inn). In 1851 Mr Samuel Cox changed premises again, this time to the present premises of the *Free Press* on the western side of the Royal Huntsman.

A photograph of 1901 showing Cox's shop in Fore Street.

The first edition of the *Free Press* was published on 27 July 1860. The paper was so named because of the then recent abolition of both the Paper Duty and Newspaper Advertising Duty which had created a far greater degree of freedom for the press than had been experienced previously. Not surprisingly, the name 'Free Press' was not only given to West Somerset's local paper, but to a number of others across the country.

Despite the relaxation of the above-mentioned duties, Mr Cox did not have an easy task to perform. Many influential people looked with distaste on the growing opportunities for enlightenment of ordinary folk, and the announcement that a purely local newspaper was to be published was received with a certain amount of anger – in some instances even accompanied by threats of a boycott of the proposed publication. Despite this, Mr Cox went ahead and the first copy saw the light amid considerable local interest.

Alfred Hutchings and E. Peppin were the first two apprentices to be employed at the *Free Press* offices and successive generations of the Cox family – Mr Herbert Cox (1873–1922), Mr F.N. Cox and Mr N.H.J. Cox – continued what Samuel had begun. Following the sudden death of Mr Norman Cox in November 1970, Mr Jack Hurley was appointed editor; he had trained as a journalist with the paper after leaving school and remained with the *Free Press* until retirement. The present editor at the time of writing is Mr Gareth Purcell, and the paper's arrival every Friday is still eagerly awaited by its many readers in West Somerset and further afield.

Like every newspaper the *Free Press* has had its anxious moments, not least during the war years. Of particular note was the occasion when the press broke down and the paper only proceeded to print thanks to the innovative help of Gliddons (see page 49). In 1959, owing to the national printers' strike, the *Free Press* was forced to print in a much reduced format.

Almost without exception, however, the *Free Press* has been well served by a very loyal and reliable workforce, many of whom stayed with the company for their entire working lives and gave outstanding service. The old compositors and mechanical typesetters would now be amazed if they saw how modern technology with computer typesetting and illustrating has changed production methods.

The *Free Press* is now owned by the Tindle Newspaper Group based in Farnham, Surrey, and is printed away from Williton, but the staff still occupy its local premises and provide West Somerset folk with their weekly newspaper every Friday without fail.

SHORT NOTICE.

GRAND ENTERTAINMENT

The CANDIDATES selected for the Parish Council, Williton,
will give a Grand Entertainment in a

TENT made out of Election Canvas,

And erected in a FIELD, known as

BATTLEGORE,

ON

DECEMBER 32nd (NOT BEING LEAP YEAR),

And the following Classic Programme will be given.

Song ... ... "Old John Barleycorn" ... John Mashtun.
Duet ... ... "All's Well" Peter Pumphandle & Tom Rosebud.
With Tin-pan Accompaniment by Mr. Ben Liddon.
Song ... ... "Let me dream again" ... W. H. Farrier.
(With Small-tooth-Comb Obbligato by the Dry Docker).
Song ... ... "Call me back again" ... G. Billson.
Song ... ... "He dunno where 'E are" ... J. Scrubditch.
Song ... ... "Ben Bolt" ... F. B. Gassum.
Song ... ... "Was'nt that a Pull Back?" ... H. J. Squark.
Song ... "Tommy, make room for your Uncle" T. Yandrew.
Song ... ... "Johnny, get your Gun" ... J. H. Haddem.
Comic Song "I gave him a Tap in the Wes'kit" P. Spigott.
Solo ... ... "Hold the Fort" ... Alb. Witherums.
Song ... ... "The Miller of Doodle-dee" ... John Squark.
Song (with Dance) "Tarara-boom-de-ay" ... Tom Sarka.
Recitation ... "The Frog and the Ox" Peter Pumphandle.
Song ... ... "Never mind the Rest" ... Tom Rosebud.

Accompanist: PROFESSOR STRIKEHARD.

Doors open at 10; Concert to commence at 12.30 p.m. prompt.

Prices of Admission: Adults in arms, 5s.; Front Seats, Free;
Back Seats, Half-price.

Proceeds will be given to the Hospital for Incurable Jokers.

Below: *This 1960s photograph confirms that Cox Sons & Co Ltd continued to trade in updated premises in Fore Street as well as the Long Street premises until the Fore Street business was sold to Mr Mann (who then sold to Cllr H. Davies).*

Above: *Dinner to mark the centenary of the* West Somerset Free Press *held at the Egremont Hotel on 29 July 1960. At the top of the picture are: Mr N.H.J. Cox (news editor), Mr F.N. Cox (head of company and managing editor) and Mr H.A. Cox (Director).*

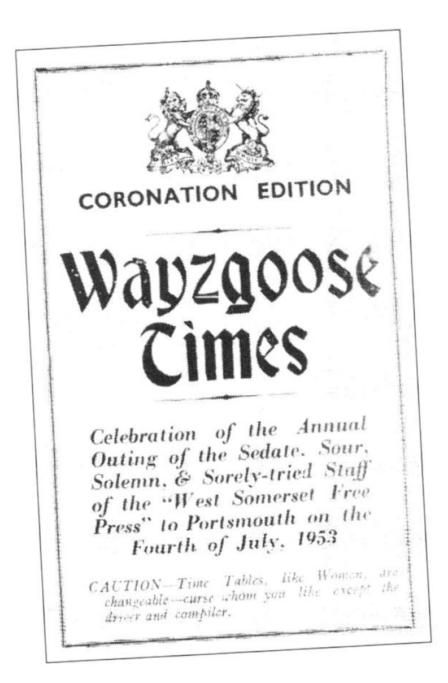

CORONATION EDITION

Wayzgoose Times

Celebration of the Annual Outing of the Sedate, Sour, Solemn, & Sorely-tried Staff of the "West Somerset Free Press" to Portsmouth on the Fourth of July, 1953

CAUTION—Time Tables, like Women, are changeable—curse whom you like except the driver and compiler.

Above: *Members of the* Free Press *staff on a 'Wayzgoose' (printers outing) in the 1920s. Well-known Williton personality Harry Burge is in the centre of the group (with buttonhole).*

Above left: *Annual* Free Press *outings were recorded by means of special editions of the* Wayzgoose Times *which often contained jokes and take-offs. Above left is the front cover of the July 1953 edition of* Wayzgoose. *On the opposite page is a spoof handbill issued by the* Free Press.

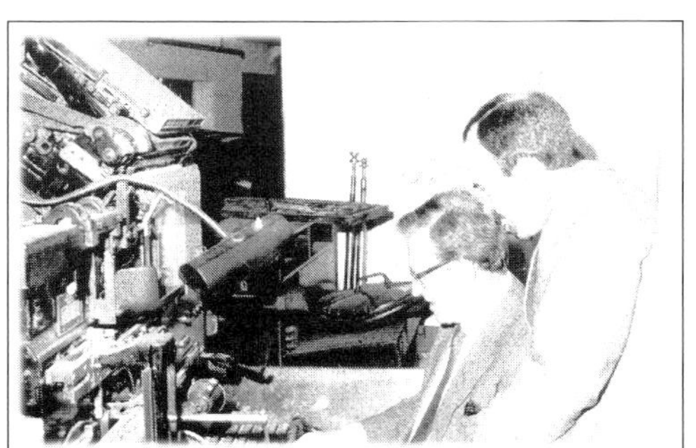

Left: *Tom King, then MP, trying his hand at the old 'hot metal' method of typesetting on a Linotype machine. With him is the* Free Press's *editor at the time of writing, Gareth Purcell.*

Free Press *Footballers, 1910.*

This picture of the old printing press shows the last issue of the paper which was printed in Williton, November 1989.

Chapter Eight

Travel & Climate

The railway came to Williton in 1862 when the line extending from a junction with the Bristol and Exeter Railway at Norton Fitzwarren to Watchet was completed. The wide-gauge line was later extended to Minehead (c.1874) which further improved communication and services to Williton. Conversion of the whole length of the line (23 miles) to standard gauge took place in 1882. The line was first worked by the Bristol and Exeter Railway, then by the Great Western Railway, and played a major role in the development of Minehead as a resort (see *The Book of Minehead with Alcombe*).

Nationalisation of the railways took place in 1947, but just over two decades later in 1971 the branch line was closed. The Mayor of Taunton greeted the Chairman of Minehead Urban Council for a formal ceremony at Taunton and Williton schoolmasters David Beach and John Holroyd wrote a song 'Last Train' to mark the occasion. Representatives of the Rural District Council were at Williton Station to give the train a suitable send off and the *Free Press* gave full coverage under the headline 'BOWLERS AND BLACK FOR LAST RESPECTS'.

In that same year, West Somerset Railway Ltd became a private company and, thanks to the hard work of numerous dedicated volunteers, still exists today, operating between Bishops Lydeard and Minehead and serving all stations between. It is also hoped to re-establish a permanent link with the main line in the near future so that operations will begin once again between Taunton and Minehead.

The arrival of the railway at Williton brought with it a new bridge which crossed the line and carried the main road into the village. This structure, known as Highbridge, gave its name to the nearby nursery house of the Martin family (formerly Jones) and the garden adjoining the station platform provides an attraction for passengers and visitors.

The photograph *2nd from top on page 8* showing the flooded roadway at the foot of the Highbridge also shows two cottages facing into the road. These cottages were later burnt down due to a spark from a steam-driven lorry and demolished to make way for two bungalows which were built for Mr H. Martin. The passenger station at Williton with a gated road crossing overlooks the nursery house and gardens, but on the other side, which is close to the trading estate, are adjoining extensive engineering facilities for both steam and diesel engines. Year after year volunteers come from near and far to spend working holidays here enjoying the railway, and a journey on the West Somerset Railway is an event enjoyed by many thousands each season. As a bonus to all enthusiasts, the railway is also home to the Somerset and Dorset Railway Museum which can be found at Washford Station.

Top: *The former mineral line at nearby Watchet.* (Courtesy James Date Archive)
Above: *Flooding at Williton Station.*

West Somerset Free Press

SOUVENIR ISSUE

FRIDAY, MARCH 26th, 1976

RE-OPENING OF THE WEST SOMERSET RAILWAY

Mr. Douglas Fear, of Taunton, chairman of the West Somerset Railway Company.

Rail Chairman's Message

Mr. Douglas Fear, chairman of the West Somerset Railway, has written the following message for our readers:

The opening of the first section of the Taunton to Minehead Railway on the 28th March will be an exciting occasion I am sure for many hundreds of people in West Somerset and also in other parts of the country.

To begin with the service will operate between Minehead and Blue Anchor, but will be progressively extended during the season, and hopefully, by the end of the year a through service will be running to Taunton.

Since the present private Company was formed almost five years ago negotiations have been constantly in progress to solve the many problems encountered in the re-opening of the railway as a private undertaking. It is gratifying now to feel that the task has been successfully completed.

Considerable effort has been subscribed by the Directors of the Company and members of the West Somerset Railway Association voluntarily, and I must admit that there have been times that have been discouraging, but one particular aspect that we have always found inspiring has been the degree of enthusiasm and goodwill displayed by the public towards the success of the campaign. In many respects we are now concluding the first episode of the re-opening of the railway.

We have always made it clear that if our efforts were successful and the railway became operational its future success would depend entirely on public support. We, therefore, hope that those who have supported the campaign will make full use of the railway now it has become operational.

The present private Company is being converted to a public Company, thereby inviting members of the public to be shareholders in the company.

The redevelopment of the railway will touch the lives of all who live in West Somerset. It will also provide a great deal of technical and historical interest to railway enthusiasts everywhere.

In addition to providing a public transport service its success will open up new social and leisure interests and bring considerable economic benefits to the district. When fully operational the line will be the longest privately owned railway in the country and the only private railway offering an all year round daily public passenger service. The re-instatement and operation of the railway is a very sizeable task involving a heavy financial commitment, but with your support we feel this can and will be done. I therefore invite you to join with us by becoming shareholders of what is now your own railway.

2 WEST SOMERSET FREE PRESS SUPPLEMENT

SUCCESS TO THE LINE

The "West Somerset Free Press" has pleasure in issuing this pictorial souvenir of the re-opening of the West Somerset Railway, or, as it was commonly known when linked with a great rail network, the Taunton–Minehead branch.

We greet the new birth of this local line (when fully operational it will be the longest privately owned railway in the country), with a feeling of admiration for those who have achieved their purpose against the manifold odds and frustrations of the five years that have elapsed since we sadly chronicled the run of the "last train" in January, 1971.

Last train it certainly would have been but for the spirit and tenacity of the few—attributes that were to prove infectious in drawing together a veritable army of support for the line's revival.

However, even unwearying will and work would have been unavailing but for a significant factor. After the "last train" had gone the rails remained. That they were not taken up with the almost indecent haste that followed other railway closures was due to a "saving condition of closure" suggested in 1968 by Mr. John Peyton, then Minister of Transport. It was that the track remain intact for at least two years after the trains had ceased to run—and it was adopted.

Beating in the British breast is, we think, a strange inbred enthusiasm for railways, so that the only sure way of killing one is to take up the track. Thus we may say that the Taunton–Minehead line was never dead. It has been sleeping the seasons while the primroses have bloomed five times in the cuttings and now, with the spring, it awakens.

We tender hearty congratulations to the West Somerset Railway Company, formed in 1971, and to their host of supporters. They have succeeded in an enterprise which has confounded the defeatists and left the opponents in disarray.

The "Free Press" is two years older than the line. Samuel Cox, founder and first editor, was glad for the original enterprise that brought the railway in 1862. Now the line could deliver the newsprint which previously had come by road coach. And it was to Williton station, at the end of the week, that the finished newspaper product was taken for despatch.

And so it was for the next hundred years, through economic and social progress and the debilitating effects of two World Wars. In the "Free Press" offices, publication morning invariably meant a clock-watch—"we Must catch the train."

We could tell many a tale—for instance, how, in an excess of speed the handcart pusher forgot his braking distance and cart and papers went over the platform edge on to the line.

But this souvenir is not for "Free Press" stories. It is for stories of the line. Naturally, the bulk of its content must be retrospective. Yet we must look "up the line" futuristically and hope that it may have a long run of progressively increasing use.

Mostly, we look "down the line—back through the years, at some of its career and its characters. Privately, readers may be able to select their own favourite ghosts—from characters and voices long departed.

But perhaps the friendliest, most heart-warming ghost voice is that emanating from the old "Minehead bay" at Taunton station—"Any more for the Minehead line?"

"Yes, wait for us," many a homecomer must have responded. For this was the "last lap line"—bringing them back to old West Somerset.

So, a toast to happy recollection, and another to a new romance of rail to which next Sunday will give birth.

THE EDITOR

Mainly for steam fans

The re-opening of the line is exciting enough in itself, but the fact that it will restore steam locos to the scene is pure ecstacy in the breasts of the countless numbers of people of all ages who succumb to the majesty of steam at work. Let it be remembered that growing up is a generation of children to whom steam traction is just an occasional glimpse on old film or a picture in a book.

Victor (pictured on back page) and Vulcan are among the engines that will belch and cough in that poetry of motion and effort which has always quickened the heartbeats of the steam enthusiasts.

Starting, of course, in steam, the Minehead line ended in the apparently effortless diesel motive power which had been introduced in the early 1960s.

Although the new company's plans provide in due course for a diesel commuter service between Minehead and Taunton, the use of steam locos will give the line a captivating character. Those locos will pull more than trains; they will be sheer magnetism for tourists.

The old line's steam traction lasted roughly 100 years. The early engines, ugly brutes lacking the symmetry of their descendants, gradually gave way to a small saddle tank type dubbed the "Minehead tiddler"; then more powerful tank and also tender engines were used, but rarely were any named locos seen on the branch. The few included members of the bird-name 2–4–0 "Bulldog" class—Seagull, Chaffinch, Cormorant, Kingfisher and Penguin.

Chaffinch became the pride of the women cleaners at Taunton during the war; they always turned her out with a beautifully polished name-plate.

The young collectors of engine names nearly had others for their notebooks. After the war consideration was given to using G.W.R. "Manor" class engines (108 tons) on the line, but it was decided that they were unsuitable, and nothing larger than the 4300 class of 2–6–0s was ever allowed, even for the Duke of Edinburgh's royal train to Minehead in 1952.

True, one monster loco, the Duchess of Hamilton, came down the line in 1964 to spend some ten years as a show piece at Butlin's Minehead camp, but she was towed "dead," and even then there were sighs of relief when she reached Minehead without mishap.

Minehead
Service Station
wish every success to the
West Somerset
Railway Company
BUT EVEN WITH THE RAILWAY, YOU WILL STILL NEED A CAR — COME ALONG AND SEE OUR WIDE RANGE OF
NEW VAUXHALL & FIAT CARS
FOR IMMEDIATE DELIVERY
ALSO LARGE STOCK OF
QUALITY TESTED USED CARS

Townsend Road, Minehead
Telephone 3379/3238

Less than two minutes walk from the Railway Station
C. W. Richardson & Co.
Auctioneers and Estate Agents
29, The Avenue
Minehead
Telephone 3212/3
Wishing the
West Somerset
Railway Company
every success in their venture

BUTLINLAND
MINEHEAD
wish the
West Somerset
Railway
EVERY SUCCESS
for a
PROFITABLE FUTURE

Left and below: *Mr and Mrs George B. Gadd standing beside their touring car, which was also available for hire. Mr Gadd was licensee of the Wyndham Arms Hotel and enjoyed the distinction of being only the second man in Somerset to be awarded a driving licence. He was also one of the first motorists to pass an examination in the mechanism, driving and general management of motor cars in 1907. This he achieved most satisfactorily under the auspices of The Motor Drivers Union Ltd. His certificate is reproduced below.*

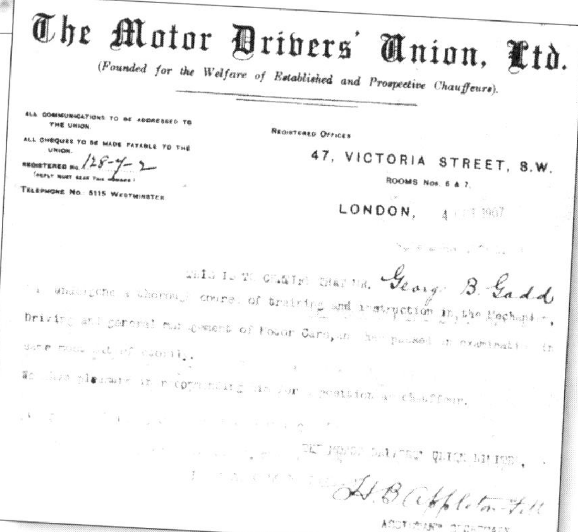

The Motor Drivers' Union, Ltd.

(Founded for the Welfare of Established and Prospective Chauffeurs).

ALL COMMUNICATIONS TO BE ADDRESSED TO THE UNION.
ALL CHEQUES TO BE MADE PAYABLE TO THE UNION.
REGISTERED No. 128-7-2
(REPLY MUST BEAR THIS NUMBER)
TELEPHONE No. 5115 WESTMINSTER

REGISTERED OFFICES
47, VICTORIA STREET, S.W.
ROOMS Nos. 6 & 7.
LONDON, [illegible] 1907

THIS IS TO CERTIFY THAT Mr. George B. Gadd [illegible] course of training and instruction in the Mechanism, Driving and general management of Motor Cars, [illegible] passed [illegible] examination [illegible]

We [illegible] pleasure in recommending him for [illegible] position [illegible] chauffeur.

[illegible] MOTOR DRIVERS' UNION LIMITED,

H. B. Appleton-Fill
ASSISTANT SECRETARY.

Above: *Here new-fangled motor cars mix with horse-drawn transport outside the Egremont, c.1920s.*

Bradbeer's Garage was one of the first establishments to cater for motor vehicles in Williton.

Public Transport

The well known and highly regarded company of Bryants Coaches was founded by the late Mr E.G. Bryant, of the Notley Arms, Monksilver, in 1932. The business started with driven cars for hire, then larger vehicles, followed by buses. With the expansion of the business, the company moved to a site in Station Road, Williton, in the late 1930s, where their depot remains to this day. During the war years the firm was very active in transporting local workers to and from the munitions factory at Puriton, near Bridgwater. Over many years the company has given a much appreciated and reliable service to the people of West Somerset, and has also ferried thousands of children to and from schools in the area. Bryant's modern fleet of coaches operates tours and private trips throughout the year, increasing in number during the summer months.

The company also runs holiday coach tours to various parts of Britain and Ireland and some to the Continent. The firm is noted for its personal, friendly and courteous service and has been fortunate in having a wonderful record for helpful staff, many of whom have given many years of dedication to the job.

Above: *A mishap with the bus in North Road, March 1962.*

Right: *Three of the line of Bryants Coaches long-service drivers, left to right: Gordon Dennett, Stan Dunn and Brian Dennett – with 120 years' service between them!*

Left: *Group travel was rather different in the days of the charabanc. Here Members of the* Free Press *staff are seen setting out on one of their annual 'Wayzgoose' excursions during the 1920s.*

Climate

Sheltered by hills, Williton enjoys a moderate climate and is rarely affected by extremes of weather, but of course storms do occur. In the late 1700s and early 1800s flooding was a common problem and Long Street and North Street were badly affected – although this was as much due to a lack of drainage as bad weather. Heavy snowfalls are rare and the three falls of note recorded in the last century were in 1922, 1947 and 1962–63.

Top: *St Peter's in the snow, 1962.*

Above: *Long Street snow scene, taken on 1 April 1922.*

Above: *Bridge Street, 1922.*

Right: *The Taunton Road at Woolston, January 1963.*

Left: *On Thursday 12 July 1900, the village was hit by a severe storm of heavy rain and hailstones. The morning was very hot but by midday clouds had developed and within a short space of time it became very dark. Flashes of lightning were followed by a fall of hail, and after a short while the full fury of the storm broke, sending down a very heavy fall of hailstones which varied from walnut size to over 2 inches in diameter, and caused considerable damage to skylights, greenhouses and windows. Skylights at the Egremont Hotel were damaged and 100 panes of glass were broken at the Workhouse. The storm was short-lived but left roads covered with thick ice, and flooding of properties followed as the ice thawed. This photograph shows a collection of hailstones one hour after they had fallen.*

In January 1901 Williton and the surrounding area was under siege from widespread flooding, with houses in Robert Street under water. Doniford residents were forced to clear their furniture outside as they struggled to cope with the deluge. Many homes were submerged under a foot of water and roads were turned into canals. A century on and Robert Street residents and others in Williton are once again being subjected to flooding on a similar scale.

Above: *Flooding in Long Street, 12 June 1924.*

Right: *Flooding in the Doniford Road during the 1920s.*

St Peter's School, c.1940.

St Peter's School staff, 1948.
Left to right, back: Mr H. Armstrong, Mr R.V. Garland, Mr Darby, Mr A.L. Kinsey, Miss Chilcott, Mr G.H. Fry; front: Mrs E. Trebble, Miss M. Venables, Mr L.A. Lang, Mr W.J. White (headmaster), Miss Tovey, Mrs A. Osborne, Miss V.M. Davis

Chapter Nine

Education

One of Williton's early schools is thought to have been founded by the Countess of Egremont and some classes were held in teachers' homes. The schoolhouse, built during the 1830s, has been extended over a period of time and has been used as Williton Social Club since 1930. It also served as a men's club until ladies were admitted during the 1970s.

The Junior School was built in Bridge Street in 1872 and over the years this school was supplemented by additional outbuildings to accommodate increasing numbers of pupils until it was replaced by the purpose-designed school in Doniford Road. The old school is now used as offices for Magna West Somerset Housing Association.

A large Secondary School was built in North Road during 1957, and this school later became Williton Middle School, now known as Danesfield C. of E. Community Middle School.

The new St Peter's First School in Doniford Road, which replaced the outdated Victorian school at the other end of the village, was officially opened by the Bishop of Taunton, the Rt Revd Richard Lewis, on 28 February 1996. The Bishop, fully robed for the occasion, met up with pupils, staff, parents, governors and county education chiefs to celebrate the new £655 000 school. He was given a tour of the school by its head, Mrs Valerie Ellis, and talked to the children in the classrooms. The school hall was packed with over 200 people, including Somerset's Chief Education Officer and the county's Education Committee Chairman, for the opening service, which was conducted by the Vicar of St Peter's, the Revd Richard Allen. The Chairman of Govenors, Dr Bob Rivett, gave a speech about the importance of the school to the community and after the service children and staff were presented with commemorative coins paid for by St Peter's PTA.

Williton's long-awaited new County Secondary School, situated north of the Masons Arms on the Watchet road, was opened in January 1957 under the headmastership of Mr L.A. Witham, with Mr R.V. Garland as deputy headmaster, and Mr K.C. Weedy as Chairman of Governors.

The new school had its official opening with due ceremony in June 1957 by the then Lord Mayor of London, Sir George Cullem Welch. The event was also attended by many county and local education officials and other dignatories. Hundreds of parents and children had a glimpse of London-style old-world pageantry, for accompanying the Lord Mayor were the Lady Mayoress and the Lord Mayor's Serjeant at Arms and Sword Bearer, Commander John Poland. Also present was a footman.

The anniversary of the day was in future years to be known locally as the Lord Mayor of London's Day. The school's large hall, complete with stage, has been a great asset to the village over the years and is still used by many local organisations for concerts, plays, public meetings, etc. The school is named Danesfield in view of its close proximity to the fields of Battlegore where a gory battle against the invading Danes was thought to have been fought centuries earlier in 918.

A list of Williton schoolteachers for the period 1939–56 survives and reads as follows:

Pre-war teachers: *W.J. White (headmaster), Miss Tovey, Ron Garland, Miss Smith, Miss Huggins, Miss Spry, Mr Cluett.*
Wartime teachers: *Miss Bladon, Miss Boatright (Mrs Turner), Mr Daniels, Mr Horsman (woodwork), Edna Trebble, Miss Ashworth, Mrs Legge, Verna Davis (Mrs Notley).*
Post-war teachers: *Aubrey Lang, Harry Armstrong, Hugh Fry, Laurie Kinsey, Mr Moffatt, Mr Darby (woodwork), Mr Brown (woodwork), John Thomas, Tony West, Chas Bye, Phil Wheatley (Mrs Ashman), Jessie Battye (Mrs Norman), Connie Bell, Mary Venables (Mrs Robertson), Anne Dobson, Mrs Barber, Miss Chilcott, Anne Osborne, Marjory Coles, Miss Taverner.*
Dinner ladies: *Joan Baker, Mrs Cridge, Mrs Grandfield, Mrs Hardacre, Mrs Bulpin, Mrs Buller.*
Caretakers: *Mr Watts, Arnold Bedell, Jack Perry.*
Groundsman: *Mr Haytor.*
Secretaries: *Mrs Venn, Mrs Lovelace.*

St Peter's School, Standards 1 and 2, c.1948. Left to right, back: S. Nethercott, J. Hutchings, K. Buller, S. Lock, V. Howard, J. Pope, R. Thomas, J. Tipper, P. Bellringer; 3rd row: M. Tremlett, P. Williams, B. Hayes, ?, R. Peppin, W. Chidgey, C. Parberry, D. Taylor; 2nd row (seated): A. Trebble, I. Palfrey, G. Cubbins, C. Bowden, Mrs Osborne, B. Peppin, R. Webber, E. Dunn, M. Ashman; front: D. Trebble, C. Grandfield, W. Luck, A. Chilcott, D. Howells.

St Peter's School, Standards 3 and 4, 1948. Left to right, back: S. Trebble, J. Ford, V. Sully, J. Carvell, A. Chilcott, J. Burnell, I. Ford, M. Beaver; middle: ?, C. Brewer, D. Chidgey, D. Hunt, C. Chidgey, ?, R. Wood, G. Haller, B. Hayes; front: P. Payne, D. Davis, ?, J. Winter, Mrs E. Trebble, J. Pope, J. Walford, P. Perry, F. Merson; on ground: R. Lyddon.

St Peter's School Juniors, c.1950.
The teachers are Miss Chilcott (left) and Miss M. Venables.

St Peter's School Field Handball Team, 1937–38.
Left to right, back: F. Cheek, M. Tarr, P. Hughes, M. Bale, Y. Bourne, J. Sweet, D. Sully;
front: M. Trebble, R. Bale, P. Street, E. Tudball, J. Bennett.

Top: *Children enjoy the Jubilee, 1935.*

Above: *One of the Williton School Coronation pageant tableaux, 1953. Left to right: Sonia Knight, Brenda Morgan, Joyce Chave, Barbara Fry, Ruth Tooze, Jean Pope.*

Right: *Singing for Williton School at the Regal Theatre, Minehead, c.1952. From left: Malcolm Ashman, Ruth Larwood, John Branchflower, Dawn Baker.*

Top: *County School staff, 1957. Left to right, back: Mr G.H. Fry, Mr Burton, Mr A.L. Kinsey, Mr C. Bye, Miss Tovey, Mrs Barber, Mr L.A. Witham (headmaster), Mrs P. Ashman, Mr J. Toal, Mrs M. Coles, Mr H. Armstrong; front: Mr A. West, Mr L. Rowe, Mr J.H. Thomas, Mr R.V. Garland.*

Above: *Danesfield School music pupils, December 2000.*

Left: *Danesfield C of E School.*

Williton Court Leet held its last meeting in 1953. The Court was held at the New Inn (now the Royal Huntsman Inn) in Long Street. The Court Leet usually met at or around Michaelmas when they would eat a Michaelmas goose and drink their rather potent Michaelmas punch. The recipe for this has always been, and still is, a well-kept secret, handed down from licensee to licensee.

CHAPTER TEN

Keeping the Peace & Armed Forces

COURT LEET

The Court Leet or Moot dates back to Saxon times and was set up to keep law and order and look after the interests of the manor. It has unfortunately lapsed in recent times but annual meetings took place at the New Inn (now the Royal Huntsman). Only formal business was done as the court had no actual powers. The 12 jurymen were summoned by the Court bailiff and the proceedings were conducted by the lord of the manor. The jurymen took a solemn oath of allegiance to the sovereign and lord of the manor and after being sworn in on the Bible two inspectors of weights and measures, a water bailiff, two ale-tasters and a hayward were appointed.

The last meeting of the Court Leet in Williton took place in 1953 on the presentment of the Jury with a view to pledge to George Colville Wyndham Esq, held at Williton, on Wednesday 28 October 1953 by George Nöel Hinton, steward. The last action taken by the court was a letter to Williton Rural District Council in 1934 in which it was written: 'We present the bad condition of the footpath at Williton especially in Long St and request the WRDC to have the same put in a better and safer condition.'

The following is a reproduction of a summons to attend the last Williton Court Leet in 1953:

Manors of Williton Regis, Williton Hadley And Williton Fulford in the County of Somerset
to Mr Henry Hole
I hereby summon and warn you to appear at the Court Leet with a view of Frank pledge of George Colville Wyndham Esq at the New Inn within the said manors on Wednesday the 28th day of October instant, by 12 o'clock in the forenoon precisely, to serve our Sovereign Lady the Queen and the Lord of the said Leet: and herein fail not at your peril.

Given under my hand this day 22nd October 1953

H.H. Hole, Bailiff of the said court.

This had to be delivered by hand to all jurymen by the bailiff. The jurymen were:

THE LORD OF THIS LEET

PERCY HUTCHINGS	CHARLES F. KILLICK
ERNEST L. WILLIAMS	JOHN E. HURLEY
HENRY HOLE	LEWIS BALE
WILLIAM J. WHITE	THOMAS WARREN
WILLIAM HURLEY	EDWIN G. CONIBEER
CYRIL C. RICHARDS	HARRY ISAAC
EDGAR W. FARMER	NORMAN H.J. COX

The document continues:

First we present several tything men, jurors, resciants within the said Leet who have made default in not appearing at this court to perform their respective suits and services.

Also we present John E. Hurley and Cyril C. Richards to be inspectors of weights and measures for the year ensuing and until others are chosen in their stead. Also we present Lewis Bale and Thomas Warren to do the office of Bailiff for the year ensuing.

We present William Chilcott as hayward to impound all cattle and pigs found in the streets of Williton and on the highway and common grounds within the jurisdiction of this Leet and then to detail the same until the damages for impounding the above for every bullock, horse, ass or pig not exceeding 2, 3 pence and for sheep and lambs, 8 pence per 20 as well as turnpike toll if he has paid for any.

Also we present and continue in force the established rules and regulations for watering the meadows near Williton, watered by Mamsey course from Lady Day to Michaelmas in the ensuing year.

Signed
G. Hinton.

Local photographer James Date, who served on the jury with the Court Leet in 1844.
He is pictured here in his Watchet studio.
(Courtesy James Date Archive)

EXTRACTS FROM COURT LEET RECORDS

1711	*We present James Plowcock to be taken tenant for Egrove Mills by having purchased the same of Mrs Burts of Dunster, whose husband had it from Mr Lucewete.*
1732	*We present Richard Amery the butcher for throwing bullock dung and other dung in Long St, which is a great nuisance to the inhabitants of the village.*
1843	*We present a pool behind George Bacon's house in Half Acre as a nuisance to the neighbourhood.*
1846	*We present the water course in Shutgate St as being dangerous and ought to be covered.*
1848	*We present the open gutter in Long St is a nuisance and danger to the public and ought to be covered.*
1869	*We present the open drain in Bridge St as a public nuisance.*
1892	*We present the state of the turnpike road and public footpath through High St and Bridge St to be out of order and dangerous to the public.*
1926	*We present the pound in Long St could be let so that it may be put to some useful purpose as it has not been used for impounding stock for some years.*

AT THE COURT SITTING ON 3 OCTOBER 1740, SIR WILLIAM BART, LORD OF THE MANOR, HAD THE FOLLOWING JURORS PRESENT:

Philip Risdon
Andrew Torrington
William Williams
George Govett
Samuel Yandle
Richard Greenslade
John Farthing
William Sully
William Mills
Thomas Coles
Roger Escott
Robert Holcombe
Thomas Washer

AT THE COURT SITTING IN 1844, WHEN THE RIGHT HON. GEORGE EARL OF EGREMONT WAS LORD OF THE MANOR, THE JURORS WERE:

Joel Thorne
James Date
Andrew Hosegood
William Date
John Stoate
George Strong
William Cridland
William Pole
James Thristle
John Leigh
Joseph Williams
Robert Langdon
Joseph Cape
Andrew Torrington
Robert Bellamy
Edward Risdon
James Bindon

THE COURT SITTING IN 1945 UNDER THE LORD OF THE MANOR WILLIAM WYNDHAM HAD MR LOVE AS STEWARD AND THE FOLLOWING AS JURORS:

Harry Ward
William J. White
Thomas Warren
Walter G. Hole
Ronald Gliddon
John Woolley
Comdo Wood
M. Vigar Langdon
Edward Farmer
Percy Hutchings
Tom Moorman
Sydney Richards
Benjamin Casson
Frederick Woolley
Ernest Williams

Tented Camp at Torweston, May 1906

Because of their smaller numbers, the Yeomanry seem to have been able to select a variety of camp sites for their training. In May 1906 they camped for 17 days in a large field beside the main road to Taunton at Torweston, a mile or so to the east of Williton. Some 450 men were in the field with their mounts.
(Information taken from an article by M.H. Jones)

Tented Camp at Torweston, May 1906

Mounted recruits in the West Somerset Yeomanry.

Men of the Somerset Light Infantry waiting for the off at Williton Station, 1914.

An unidentified photograph of Williton men during the First World War.

Doniford Camp

Following the First World War, a base at Doniford was set up for anti-aircraft gun training, and the railway transported thousands of troops for training during the years 1925–38. Probably the world's first radio-controlled plane, the Queen Bee, was used for anti-aircraft gun practice at Doniford just before the outbreak of the Second World War. It was catapulted from a cliff-top site and was all kept top secret, with the Army bringing the 'top brass' and the War Minister to Doniford. During the Second World War Doniford also became the site for an important anti-aircraft radar training centre.

(See also The Book of Watchet*)*

The Hole family business was called upon to take and develop photographs at Doniford Camp and so high was the security on goings-on at the Camp that military personnel had to be present at the studio when the film was being developed. Here a group of soldiers pose on a truck outside the Holes' Long Street shop.

Savoy Broccoli Orchestra, Williton British Legion, 1920s.
Left to right, back: R.J. Clarke, V. Childs, F. Holcombe, E. Bourne, E.G. Conibeer;
middle: S. Langdon, S. Buller, Ron Farrar, H. Burge, Ray Farrar;
front: J. Coles, W.H. Ashman.

Williton British Legion cup and shield winners, 1930s.

Parades to and from Doniford Camp were a regular Sunday sight during the annual T.A. camps. These two photographs were taken on 12 July 1925.

The shop to be seen behind this impressive line-up include Holcombe's tailors and the cycle department of Bradbeer's Garage. Between the two is the sign for Risdon, Gerrard and Hosegood, Auctioneers, Estate Agents and Valuers. The notice in this doorway is advertising the auction of the 'residential estate of St Audries with 93 acres'. Further up the road is the Post Office.

Right: *In 1938 when the rumblings of war were to be heard across the land, Williton had a change of MP when a by-election was called after the constituency MP, Mr Croom-Johnson KC, was appointed a High Court judge. The man elected to take his place was Vernon Bartlett* (right), *who served as the constituency MP throughout the war years and until 1950. His main platform had been on foreign affairs and people were well aware of his anti-Hitler views.*

Issued by the Ministry of Information on behalf of the War Office and the Ministry of Home Security

STAY WHERE YOU ARE

IF this island is invaded by sea or air everyone who is not under orders must stay where he or she is. This is not simply advice: it is an order from the Government, and you must obey it just as soldiers obey their orders. Your order is "Stay Put", but remember that this does not apply until invasion comes.

Why must I stay put?

Because in France, Holland and Belgium, the Germans were helped by the people who took flight before them. Great crowds of refugees blocked all roads. The soldiers who could have defended them could not get at the enemy. The enemy used the refugees as a human shield. These refugees were got out on to the roads by rumour and false orders. Do not be caught out in this way. Do not take any notice of any story telling what the enemy has done or where he is. Do not take orders except from the Military, the Police, the Home Guard (L.D.V.) and the A.R.P. authorities or wardens.

What will happen to me if I don't stay put?

If you do not stay put you will stand a very good chance of being killed. The enemy may machine-gun you from the air in order to increase panic, or you may run into enemy forces which have landed behind you. An official German message was captured in Belgium which ran:

"Watch for civilian refugees on the roads. Harass them as much as possible."

(The above is a portion of a Government leaflet distributed in 1940)

Left and below: *Through 1938 and 1939 Ack-Ack training at Doniford intensified, ARP was organised, the Women's Land Army came into being, preparations were made to receive evacuees and in 1940 the LDV (later to become the Home Guard) commenced duty. Above is a picture of an ARP exercise in the 1940s. Below is a photograph of Williton Home Guard.*

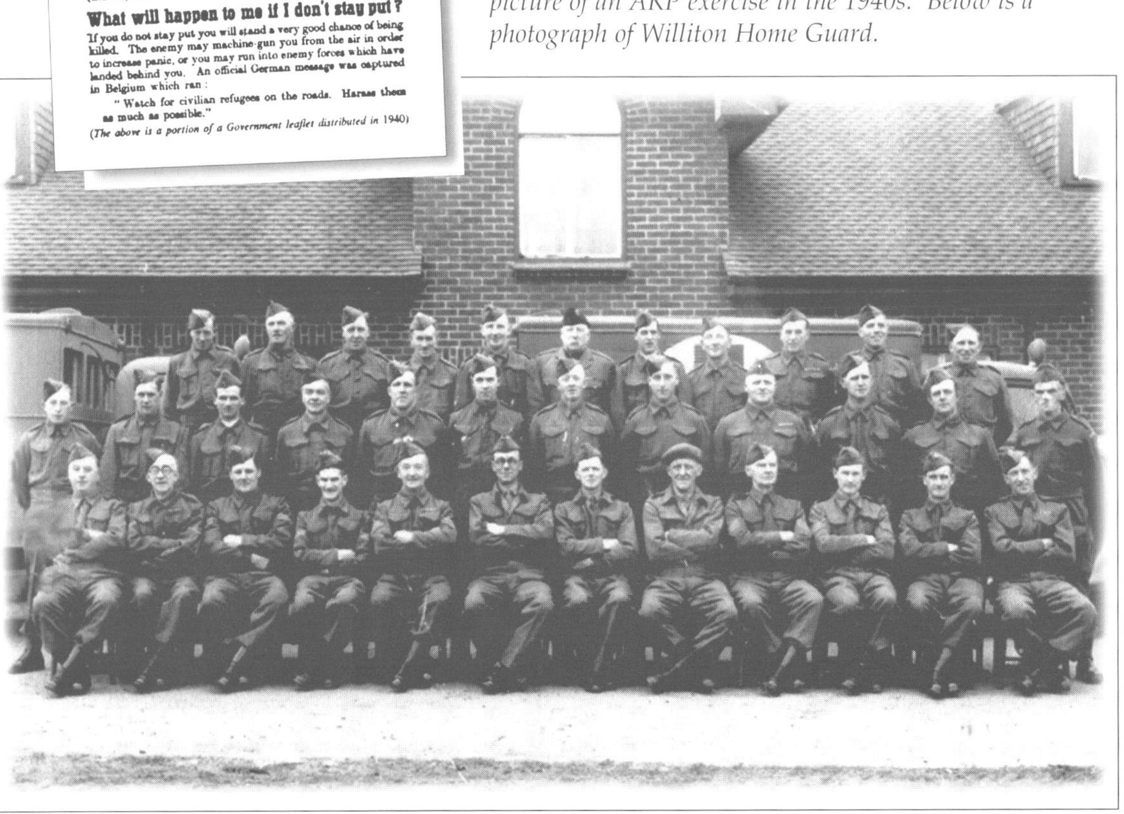

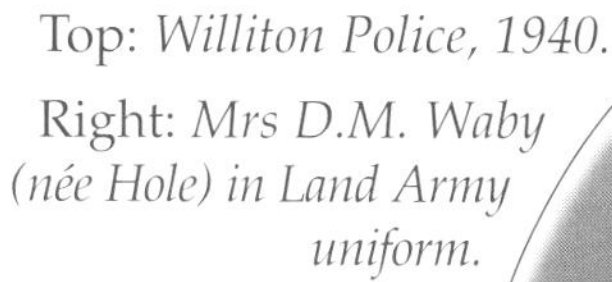

Army No

SOLDIER'S
RELEASE BOOK

CLASS "A"

Top: *Williton Police, 1940.*

Right: *Mrs D.M. Waby (née Hole) in Land Army uniform.*

Above right: *A section of a Williton Home Guard platoon. Left to right, standing: ? Banfield, T. Pearce, Laurence Chorley, W. Ashwin, R.G. Cox; front: D. Clarke, W. Scott.*

Far right: *At the beginning of the Second World War, Williton was the detraining station for evacuees directed to the area.*

Williton Symphony Orchestra in 1910.

The Mystery Jazzers including the Misses Eno, Clarke, Pullin, Bellamy, Brice and Boyles.

CHAPTER ELEVEN

Organisations & Activities

WILLITON SOCIAL CLUB

Williton Social Club has a history which goes back to the early 1900s, when a Captain Palmer opened a Reading Room for men to use in the evenings to play rings, cards and dominoes, etc. The premises had originally been the first day school in Williton. After the First World War a subscription of five shillings (25p) per year was payable (paid in two instalments, as the whole amount was too much for the average working man to pay at one time). It was known from then on as The Men's Club, and the late Mr A.T. Love and the late Mr R.E. Jackman played a prominent part in its progress. At the end of the Second World War a bar was opened. The late Mr W.J.D. Venn, an ex-postman, became the first steward, and among others who came later were Mr Chris Winter and the late Mr Ted Parrett.

The club buildings have changed over the years and, with adjoining land, were purchased from the Wyndham Estate for £100. The first skittles alley was built out of a workshop used by the late Mr Percy Hembrow; one of the rooms was once a bicycle shop. Ladies were first admitted to the club in about 1970, and then only on Sunday nights when they were restricted to using only one room! The group then became known as the Williton Social Club.

In 1980 the club underwent major alterations, during which the interior was almost completely rebuilt and refurbished, with a new bar being added. After weeks of work the club was officially re-opened on 10 July 1980 by the late Mr George Wyndham. Together with the committee, the club Secretary and his wife, Ray and June Atherton, gave much of their time to ensure that the work came to a successful conclusion. The main contractor was Mr Brian Bellamy, a member of an old Williton family.

From its inception, the club has been a place of leisure and entertainment. Prior to the Second World War, billiards (snooker was hardly ever played), table tennis, rings, table skittles and shove ha'penny were the most popular games, with bridge and nap being the favoured card games. The facilities have changed over the years, but the club remains a thriving focal point in the centre of the village where a large membership can relax and enjoy social companionship over a drink, a game of skittles, snooker, pool, darts, cards, etc., or just watch television. Live entertainment also takes place.

TWINNING SOCIETY

In 1982 a letter was received by Williton Parish Council from Neung Sur Beuvron in France with a view to the possibility of twinning. A sortie was made in 1983 by Sue and Charlie Knight and Heather and John Tennant to see the village and in 1984 the twinning ceremony was held in Neung Sur Beuvron. A further ceremony (with representatives *seen below*) was held in Williton in 1985, and since then a visit has been made almost every year, in one direction or another. Neung Sur Beuvron is situated in the wine region of the Loire Valley of France, 200 miles south of the Channel coast.

Above: *Signing of the Twinning Charter outside West Somerset District Council Offices, Williton, 1985. Left to right: Michael Shailer, Monique Lark, Tony Lark, Charles Quenet (Mayor), Lucien Perat, Jean Wall, Stuart Paisley, Sue Knight, Sheila Davies, Betty James, Mary Fisher, Margaret Shailer, Hugh Davies, Irene Nethercott.*

WILLITON GOOD NEIGHBOURS' CLUB

The Williton Good Neighbours' Club, run for the benefit of the over sixties, was formed in September 1957 and is still going strong today. The club was formed following exploratory work into the possibility of an organisation for the benefit of older, lonely and infirm people to take part once more in the general life of the village. The view was held that it would fulfil a long-felt want in the community; people from the surrounding area were also welcomed.

The first step was the formation of a committee representing various organisations, and the following were chosen: Mrs H.J. Chibbett (WI), Mrs Chanter (Red Cross), Mrs C. Martin (Girl Guides), Mrs F.H. Hall (MU and Young Wives), Mr W.C. Hurley (organiser), Mr J.E. Strong (British Legion), Mrs F. Bissell (St John Ambulance Brigade, St Audries), Mrs N. Bamforth, Revd F.J. Woods (Methodist Church), Revd F.H. Hall and Miss B. Symons (St Peter's Church), Mr C. Morton (Williton Hospital), Mrs Killick (Women's Section British Legion), Mr and Mrs Baker, Mr T. Chorley and Mr Warburton.

The inaugural meeting of the Good Neighbours' Club took place on 15 October 1957 and was well supported by a splendid attendance. At first it was suggested that the club should be called the Over Sixties, but this was changed to the Good Neighbours as members felt it was more suitable. The club's first officers to be elected were: President, Mr A.H. Stoate; Chairman, Mr N. Bamforth; Vice-Chairman, Mr F. Ware; hon. Secretary, Mr A.G. Powell; hon. Treasurer, Mr J.H. Deacon.

Meetings were initially to be held fortnightly at the Guide Hut. The club's first outing was to Lynmouth. At its first annual general meeting in November 1958 it was reported that the club had been far more successful than anyone could have expected with a membership of 120, and was hoping to move into larger accommodation for its regular meetings. Since those early days the club has gone from strength to strength, providing many happy hours of entertainment, pleasure and companionship for its members with meetings and excursions.

Above: *An early gathering of the Good Neighbours' Club.*

Right: *For its silver jubilee in 1982 the club presented a seat for use at Danesborough View. Seated in the centre and wearing her chain of office is Cllr Mrs Eileen Woods. At the back are Jack Hurley and Cllr Fred Hutchings.*

Above: *Williton Girls' Training Corps, June 1945. Left to right, back: M. Ashman, V. James, M. Williams, P. Trebble, J. Stevens, J. Sansom, M. Mogford; middle: J. Williams, D. Conibeer, J. James, B. Criddle, J. Hutchings, M. Moore, J. White, J. Burnell; front: M. Davis, E. Clarke, J. Hunt, B. Luck, M. Bale, Mrs E. Trebble, F. Gardner, J. Chorley, B. Chapman, B. Bryant, P. Dunn.*

Left: *Air Training Corps Cadets parade, 1970s.*

RED CROSS

The modern Red Cross building in Killick Way is well used not only by its own membership, but also for other gatherings, many of which are in some way associated with the work of the Red Cross. The ladies of the Women's Institute hold their weekly market in the building.

AIR TRAINING CORPS

Set up as a cadet force during the Second World War, the Air Training Corps also has a training centre building of its own in Williton, which is next door to the Church Room. The Williton ATC is part of 1013 Quantock Squadron and has been well served over the years by, among others, the late Mr Norman Jones, the late Mr Ron Slade (OBE), the late Mr Ernest Duckett and Mr Bill Court. Cadets are seen smartly turned out at various ceremonial occasions, sometimes with their standard carried alongside that of the Royal British Legion and establishing a link between past and present.

GFS

Perhaps one of the oldest organisations for girls in Williton was the Girls' Friendly Society which met in the hall behind the Post Office, previously used by Methodists as their local church from the 1820s until their new church was built at Tower Hill in 1883. The Post Office Hall seems to have enjoyed many uses, including that of canteen and rest room for soldiers from Doniford Camp during the Second World War.

Women's Institute party, 1950, at the Egremont.

Present-day requirements are such that persons involved in the preparation of food have to acquire suitable hygiene training. The ladies photographed with Roy of Coronation Street fame have completed their course and are displaying their certificates. Left to right: Becky King, Mary Brown, Mary Slade, 'Roy Cropper' (David Nielson), Pam Darkin, Amelia Langdon.

Women's Institute

Fellowship, learning and understanding are the aim of many groups and organisations but it seems that the Women's Institute, without social barriers, has achieved a high degree of success in this respect which is much admired by many other organisations. Williton WI was formed in 1918 and its first President was Lady Alice Trevellyan of Nettlecombe, who remained in office for many years. The Williton Branch, which is one of the oldest in the county, is part of the Severn Sea Group and is part of the Somerset County Federation of Women's Institutes. Meetings are held on the first Thursday of each month (except August) at the Red Cross Centre at 2p.m. and a market is held at the Red Cross Centre on Fridays at 10a.m.

Williton WI members celebrate (from top to bottom) the 50th, 70th, 75th and 80th anniversaries of the Williton Branch. Long-serving and past President Mrs V. Chibbett can be seen at each celebration.

The members present at the pictured anniversary celebrations are: 50th anniversary, left to right: Mrs Deacon (Secretary), Mrs Bowker (past President), Mrs Salter (a founder member cutting cake), Miss Bushen (past President), Mrs Colquhoun (President), Mrs Harding-Francis (county President), Mrs Rait (past President), Mrs Chibbett (past President).

70th anniversary (past Presidents). Members include: Mrs V. Chibbett, Mrs L. Garner, Mrs E. Colquhoun, Mrs N. Linck, Mrs Brown, Mrs J. Barber, Mrs M. Fisher and President Mrs V. Richards.

75th anniversary, left to right: Ann Mumford and Diana Chalk (voluntary county organisers), Joyce Hudson (President), Lilian Garner and Violet Chibbett (past Presidents).

80th anniversary, left to right: Jean Barbour (Treasurer), Wyn Williams (minute Secretary), Jean Hill, Brenda Sherman (President), Violet Chibbett (past President), Elizabeth Pilcher (longest serving member).

Cookery Class outside the GFS Hall, c.1924. Left to right, back: Florrie Chorley, Mollie Gadd, Vera Sawyer, Doris Rich, Nellie Appleby, Joan Langdon, Rene Besley; middle: Miss Tyte (teacher), Phyllis Duddridge, Gwen Guest, Mildred Bray, Joyce Boyles, Norah Ashman; front: Peggy Beare, Maisie Salter, Ivy Burge.

Church Young Wives in the early 1950s. Left to right, back: Mrs B. White, Mrs P. Sully, Mrs T. Cooke, Mrs H. Hall, Mrs B. Fry, Mrs M. Coles, Mrs L. Garland, Mrs Penny, Mrs D. Chedzoy, Mrs Doble, Mrs E. Western, Mrs D. Stockwell, Mrs M. Steer, ?, Mrs J. Parsons, Mrs J. Woods; front: Mrs I. Peppin, Mrs D. Long, Mrs E. Baker, Mrs M. Stockham, Mrs P. Chilcott, Mrs M. Slade, Mrs E. Tudball, Mrs S. Long.

Williton Ladies' Keep Fit Class, 1938.
Left to right, back row: M. Gadd, L. Gadd, Gwen Pullin, M. Eno, V. Davis, B. Jones; middle: Mrs Burnett, Gladys Pullin, Miss Spry, V. Williams, B. Venn, D. Prout, M. Bowden; sitting: F. Gardner, N. Ashman, M. Bindon, G. Branchflower, D. Lane, G. Bellamy.

Above: *Left to right, back: Joan Chorley, Mary Bale, Ethel Clarke; front: Dawn Baker.*

Left: *Part of Joy Exell's Dance Troupe, c.1947. Left to right: Ann Burnett, Valerie Sully, ?, Dawn Baker, Shirley Trebble, Peggy Cridge, June Bulger.*

Left: *Guide camp at Exmouth, 1950s.*

Below: *Opening of the Guide Hut in the 1950s.*

Centre right: *Williton Guides on parade led by Mrs C. Martin, 1950s.*

Below left: *Williton Guides 75th birthday party.*

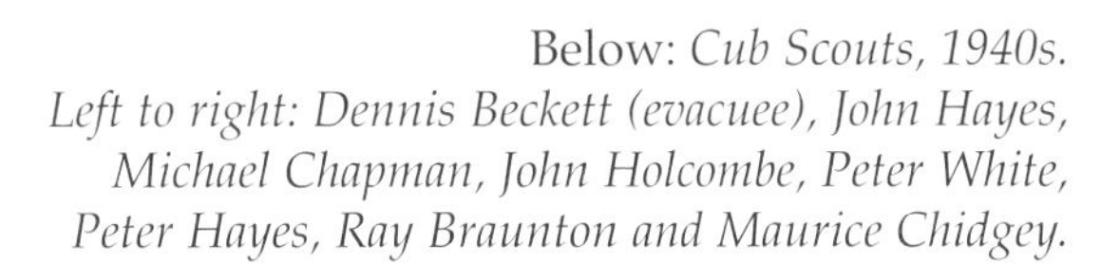

Below: *Cub Scouts, 1940s.*
Left to right: Dennis Beckett (evacuee), John Hayes, Michael Chapman, John Holcombe, Peter White, Peter Hayes, Ray Braunton and Maurice Chidgey.

Guides and Scouts

Both the Guides and the Scouts have been active in Williton for many years and even managed to continue activities during the years of the Second World War under restricted circumstances and mostly without their uniforms, as can be seen in the photograph of Cubs in the 1940s. The Guides and Scouts of today both have headquarters of their own and there is little doubt that the Cubs of the war years are pleased to know that the Scout group is seeking to update its headquarters on a new site, with facilities suitable for modern activities.

The Williton Guide Company was started in 1917 by the late Mrs Baxter (née Martin). When she was in her last term at school and a patrol leader in the School's Guide Company, the late Olave, Lady Baden-Powell (a friend of the headmistress), visited the school and asked each patrol leader to start a Guide Company in their own town or village. At Bicknoller where Mrs Baxter lived there were only about three girls of Guide age but she went to see the late Miss Heathcote, and advised her to start Guiding in Williton, as there were plenty of girls there with nothing to do. And so the 1st Williton Company was started, and continued without a break to celebrate its 50th birthday in September 1967 (the cake being cut by the late Mrs Baxter) and its 75th birthday in September 1992 (the cake then being cut by the late Miss Doris Killick, Lieutenant to Mrs Baxter in 1917).

Camping has always played a significant role in the Company's activities, and the first camp recorded was at East Quantoxhead – in those days palliasses were filled with hay to sleep on, and no doubt the Guides walked to this camp taking their tents, etc. on trek carts. Since then there have been many annual camps around the South West of England as well as visits to France and Switzerland.

During the Second World War the Guides joined the Civil Defence Messenger Service and helped with the war effort in many different ways, from collecting waste paper, horse chestnuts, toys, jam jars, books, etc., to the raising of monies for the Guide International Service Fund.

In 1945 it was realised that the Guides needed their own HQ (meetings then being held at the GFS Hall), and so money-raising efforts started for this. Two ex-Army huts were purchased, joined together and officially opened by the late Miss Jackson-Barstow (County Commissioner at that time) in 1948, and they gave many years good service, although they have since been replaced by a much larger and more modern building. Sadly the Guide Company had to be closed in the late 1990s owing to lack of leaders.

Brownies was started in about 1942 and is still flourishing with weekly meetings in the Guide headquarters. A Rainbow Unit (for younger girls) came into being in about 1990, and they also meet each week in the headquarters off Long Street, Williton. As the Brownies reach Guide age they have to travel to Watchet to become Guides, and so it is hoped that leaders will soon be found to re-open the Williton Guide Company.

Inspection of the Boy Scouts at Williton, date unknown.

RAOB Lodge Team. The Royal Antedeluvian Order of Buffaloes is a national friendly society for working men which was founded many years ago to provide financial help in times of hardship and illness, and also to arrange social gatherings. They also have a children's association. Williton used to have a very active lodge, which is now defunct; lodges still exist in West Somerset and further afield. Another friendly society which used to have a lodge in Williton was the Ancient Order of Foresters.

RAOB church parade in Priest Street, 1925.

Crafts

Williton is fortunate in having many and various skills represented within the community, and the talents found within the field of journalism help to keep us well informed. The special talents of a potter and a carver of international repute are a delight, and examples of their highly skilled work are illustrated here.

Below: *The potter, Martin Pettinger, with samples of his work* left, inset *and* below right.

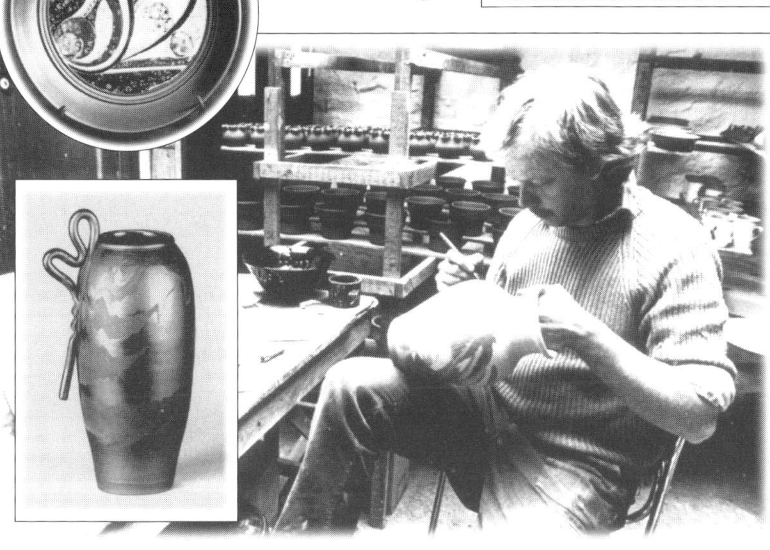

Above left and right: *Face mask carved from limewood and bonze figure with fountain head – both by Tad Mandziej.*

Right: *The late Mr Jack Chilcott, although blind, plied his skills as a basket-maker in Williton for many years. Watching studiously is his three-year-old son Arthur. Jack was a truly remarkable man.*

Williton Football Team, 1897.
Left to right, back: H. Langdon, H. Trebble, J. Holcombe;
middle: T.H. Andrew (referee), J. Durie, E. Williams, C.E. Ayres, H. Holcombe,
R.G. Upham, E.W. Page (Treasurer and Secretary);
front: D.H.A. Evans (sub Captain), A.J. Seward (Captain), A.E. Langdon, J.L. Neate.

Williton Football Team, cup and league winners, 1903–04.

Williton Football Club, Charity Cup Winners, 1924–25.
Left to right, back: F. Holcombe, L. Webber, Toby Sully, W. Branchflower, D. Routley, A. Davis, Reg Branchflower;
middle: C.H.S. Woolley, E.G. Conibeer, Rufus Sully, B. Lyddon, F.N. Cox;
front: J. Tuckfield, C. Ashman, J. Chidgey.

Williton Footballers, 1927–28.

Williton Football Club, 1952, members of the Somerset Senior League.
Left to right, back: R. Parsons, S. Terry, G. Bellamy, M. Bryant, D. Warre, B. Coleman;
front: W. Court, J.H. Thomas (County centre forward), L. Davey, K. Burnell, N. Lloyd;
mascot: Trevor Hayes.

Williton Football Team, 1965–66, Seward Cup winners.
Left to right, back: D. Sully, P. Williams, J. Holroyd, D. Chidgey, P. Armstrong, R. Sherrin, W. Calloway;
front: A. Bellamy (Secretary), R. Strong, J. Branchflower, T. Nethercott, T. Bruford, C. Norman.

Williton Cricket Team in the 1930s.
Left to right, back: S. Denning, Reg Braunton, ?, Reg Branchflower, T. Sully, Reg Date;
front: H. ('Major') Langdon, J.F. Woolley, Ray Farrar, C.H.S. Woolley, T. Branchflower;
on ground: A.L. Gliddon, J. Ashman.

Williton Cricket First Team, early 1950s.
Left to right, back: H.R. Gladwell (umpire) K. Grandfield, M. Chidgey, F. Hutchings, P. Armstrong,
J.H. Thomas, C.C. Sansom, J. Gliddon;
front: A.L. Gliddon, J.M. Sansom, H.G. Bowles, N.C. Sansom, C.T. Hann.

A 1950s 1st XI.
Left to right: R.M. Tazewell, C.T. Hann, A.L. Gliddon, P. White, Ray Braunton, K. Grandfield, M. Chidgey, G. Webber, M. England, R. Wood, J. Barber.

Williton Cricket 1st XI, 1960s.
Left to right, back: R. Coles, D. Sully, P. Hayes, D. Bendon, P. Armstrong, E. Down, D. Beach; front: Ray Braunton, K. Burnell, H. Bowles, H.G. Fry (Secretary), J. Morgan, M.Chidgey, J. Williams (scorer).

Cricket

In June 1949 Williton achieved one of its finest victories over their old cricket rivals Watchet by a margin of 76 runs. Their win was largely due to a magnificent undefeated century by opening batsman Laity Gliddon, backed by some fine bowling by Claude Hann and Bill McCord. Below is an extract from the West Somerset Free Press _which was printed following the event:_

In the local derby at Williton on Saturday the home side just beat the clock, and with only a few minutes left for play took the last Watchet wicket and scored their first victory over the seaside club for about 14 years. Williton were able to declare with 173 on the board for the loss of only five wickets, thanks to Laity Gliddon's fine 111 not out, his second century of the season, in which he was usefully partnered by Chris Sansom. Bradshaw and Pearse, especially the former, held the fort for Watchet for a long time, and Watchet nearly made a draw of it. With time running out, Claude Hann made a brilliant catch to dispose of the last man.

Williton/Watchet 1949 Cricket Scoreboard

Williton		*Watchet*	
A.L. Gliddon not out	111	F. Doble c Hutchings b Hann	1
J. Gliddon c Edwards b Ricketts	12	A. Rickets b McCord	17
C.C. Sansom b Chubb	38	A. Edwards c Hutchings b Hann	1
H.G. Bowles b Ricketts	9	O. Baker c Sansom b Hann	0
F. Hutchings b Chubb	1	J. Bradshaw c Sansom b Hann	39
C.T. Hann run out	1	A. Pearse b McCord	18
Extra	1	J. Binding b A.L. Gliddon	9
		D. Chubb l b w b McCord	0
Total (5 wickets declared)	173	D. Pugsley n.o.	10
		T. Strong b Hann	0
		R. Clavey c Hann b McCord	0
Reg Braunton, S.E. Balch, W. McCord, W.J. Barnes, C.H.S. Woolley did not bat.		Total	97
A. Rickets	2-44	C.T. Hann	5-23
D. Chubb	2-45	W. McCord	4-38
		A.L. Gliddon	1-11

Right: *All-rounder Ray Braunton.*

Below: *Williton batsmen Chris Sansom* (left) *and Laity Gliddon.*

Above: *Off-spin bowler Maurice Chidgey.*

Left: *Bowler Bill McCord.*

Railway Hotel Cup winners – Old Cleeve and District Skittle League, 1930–31, at the Foresters Arms. Left to right, back: T. Sully, J. Langdon, ?, W. Chilcott, Reg Branchflower; front: R. ('Buckley') Langdon, J.F. Woolley, A.J. ('Lord') Seward, H. ('Major') Langdon.

The Egremont Hotel 'A' Skittles Team, early 1960s. Left to right, back: D. Langdon, J. Henson, D. Sully, W. Sully, D. Clarke; front: L. Sweetland (sticker-up), Mrs W. Smith (landlady), H. Isaac (Captain), Mr D. Smith (landlord), J. Walford.

BOWLS

The Bowls Club enjoys a setting with convenient access in very pleasant surrounds and its facilities have developed with the sport. The club was founded in 1923 and the green was laid with turf brought from the Quantock Hills. Friendly rivalry exists between clubs, particularly with the club over the hill at Watchet ensuring that players make every effort to enhance their skills – the very high standard of the Williton Green is envied by some visiting players. The club Captain from 1924 until 1929 was Mr A.J. Seward, who was also the first winner of the Challenge Cup in 1928.

The ladies' section was formed during the 1970s and quickly attained high standards. The year 1977 was a triumphal one for the club when the ladies' team won the Fear Cup and the men's team won the South Somerset League Championship. The 1977 ladies included D. Covey, J. Bamforth, D. Trunks, E. Ashman, R. Knight, D. Court, F. Pattimore, L. Hayhoe, J. Grove, M. Sharpe, E. Robertson and W. Cook. The 1977 men were B. Robertson, H. Stevens, A. Hooper, K. Pattimore, W. Hayes, A. Cook, R. Bryant, C. Bruford, J. Pearson, F. Merson, S. Hensley, R. Owen, C. Takle, H. Bowen, K. Davis and A. Stone.

Left: *Captain's Day, 1999.*

Williton Bowling Club, c.1950s.
Left to right, back: J. Morton, A. Smither, A.H. Stoate, G. Hier-Evans, J. Horsman;
middle: W.J. Yandle, F. Burnett, H.C. Michell, S. Denning, R. Maunder;
front: H.J. Chibbett, F. Risdon, C.F. Clatworthy, E.J. Bale, L.H. Bryant, A.J. Seward.

Foxhounds, c.1920.

A meet of the West Somerset Foxhounds outside the Egremont, date unknown.

The Badger Seekers, 17 September 1938.

Point-to-point racing at Williton.

Coronation celebratory service and march held in Williton, 12 May 1937, an event for which the village was decorated in fine style.

Chapter Twelve

Special Events

Royal Occasions

Threatening clouds, wintry weather and showers of rain could not dampen the enthusiasm of Her Majesty Queen Elizabeth II's loyal subjects on her Coronation Day, Tuesday 2 June, 1953. Most of the day's programme in Williton, as elsewhere, took place in the afternoon as many took the opportunity never offered before of viewing the Coronation Service in Westminster Abbey and the London processions on television.

In anticipation of the great day Williton had gone gay with flags and bunting across the streets and against houses and business premises, and there was an added incentive to create a festive look as the organising committee offered prizes for the best decorated private or business premises. Notable in Fore Street was the decorative scheme of the RDC offices, including over the entrance a trellis arch with red, white and blue flowers, and at night the building was floodlit.

The day itself was a traditional one of feasting and sports for young and old, with the ladies of the catering committee bearing the brunt of the work. Funds had been raised 'on the rates' and by voluntary subscription as well. The organising committee, representative of all organisations in the village, had found an excellent secretary in Mr L.A. Lang, who had the assistance of Mr W.J. White, the able Chairman Mr H.J. Chibbett, and the hon. Treasurer Mr G.F. Clark. Heads of the various sub-committees were: Teas, Mrs N. Jones; decorations and fancy dress, the Revd Frank Hall and the Revd D. Gourlay Thomas; bonfire and fireworks, Dr C.F.R. Killick; spoons and mugs, Mr H.J. Chibbett; television, Mr H.R. Fell; and other members of the committee were Mesdames H.A. Chanter, N.G. Linck, J.M. Martin, D.M. Buee, F.R. Killick, and the Misses D. Leversha, Q. Bale, D.J. White, and S. Burnett, and Messrs F.J. Ware, G. Western, N. Jones, J.H. Thomas, H.J. Coles, V.S. Buller, S.E. Balch, R.J. Ashman, J.E. Strong and R. Peppin, with many other helpers volunteering from all organisations.

On Coronation Day there were early celebrations of Holy Communion at St Peter's and the Methodist churches. Many people took advantage of watching the London pageantry and the Abbey ceremony on television, the committee having arranged for the installation of sets by Mr E.G. (Ted) Ashman on the Recreation Ground.

Mrs Bradbeer had also provided a television at her garage premises (now the Co-op supermarket), and large numbers took advantage of these facilities as few people had TV sets in their own homes at that time. In the afternoon there was a fancy-dress parade for children, the judge being Mrs E.S. Reed. Her awards were: Children under eight, 1st Jacqueline Bedford, 2nd (equal) Jane Bedford and Anne Archer, 3rd Angela Chidgey, with highly commended awards going to Janet Chilcott, Dawn Abbott and Jean Maxfield. In the over-eight section, 1st went to Gweneth Williams, 2nd to Susan Belcher, 3rd to Sonia Gardiner, and highly commended awards to Ann Maxfield and Pauline Fletcher. For Elizabethan costumes (in the 15 and under group), 1st prize went to Jennifer Stone and Dawn Baker (equal).

A programme of sports followed in the afternoon. Before tea the vicar, the Revd Frank Hall, and the Revd D.G. Thomas presented over 300 souvenir mugs to the children. The presentation and the service of teas were carried out in relays, with adults as well as children being catered for. Later there was a tea party for the over 65s at the Church Room, which had been gaily decorated. About 60 sat down to a splendid meal. Among the happy company were Mrs Barwick and Mrs Reeves (both 89), Mr Hodges and Mr G. Salter (both 82 and Boer and First World War veterans). The happy gathering was wound up by entertainment being provided by Mrs Lovelace, Miss J. Western, Mr H. Armstrong, Miss S. Hurley and the vicar. Mrs M. Slade, Miss J. Western and Mr H. Armstrong all took turns at the piano.

At night the people had an excellent view of the bonfire which was lit on Lines, above Tower Hill, one of the highest points overlooking Williton, and also of a firework display. A late-night dance in the Church Room ended a very enjoyable and happy day. The judges for the decoration of houses and business premises were Dr M.D. Tonks and Mrs R.E. Harenc. They awarded 1st prize for decorated private house to 'Pyrcot' and 'Garhwal', adjoining premises in North Street, where the scheme, including a home-made model of the crown, had been devised by Mrs J.E. Hurley, with lighting effects by Mr F.V. Matson. Second and third respectively fell to Mrs R. Baker and Mrs Hayter. Mr F. Hutchings' premises in North Street secured the premier award in the business class, a most artistic effect being achieved in the national colours, and 2nd and 3rd prizes were won respectively by the Electricity Board and Mr G.C. Hobbs. The gay gardens prizes were won by Mrs A.W. Hosegood and Mrs J. Langdon. Villagers now look forward to celebrating Her Majesty's Golden Jubilee in 2002.

The author is indebted to the *West Somerset Free Press* for access to their files, from which much of the information for the foregoing was obtained.

Williton School's pageant of the queens, 1953.
Left to right: Iris Ford, Shirley Webber, ? (ladies in waiting), Jenny Hunt (Princess Margaret), Michael Clausen (escort), Eileen Steer (Elizabeth II), Eric Clavey (escort), George Haller (Duke of Edinburgh), Marion Clausen, Audrey Chilcott, Wendy Bulpin (ladies in waiting).

Jubilee street party, 1977.

Whit Monday during the 1920s at the Memorial Ground Gymkhana. The first major event held at the Recreation Ground was in 1922 when a Gymkhana was held on Whit Monday. The next Gymkana in 1923 was attended by approximately 2000 people who came to see some 30 shire horses and other attractions. This event was attended by the then Minister for Agriculture and competing in the sports events for boys was Harold Gimblett, who later became a famous Somerset and England cricketer.

It was the custom that a procession would form at the Recreation Ground to proceed up Long Street, and the shire horses, beautifully groomed for the occasion, were a wonderful sight, as testified by this photograph from the 1930s. Pictured at the front are Laurie Buller (left) and Douglas Langdon.

Festival of Britain
WILLITON

June 17th—23rd. 1951

Chairmen: Rev. D. Gourlay Thomas, Rev. H. Saxby, Mr. W. J. White.

Committee: Mesdames C. Martin, R. Coggins, A. E. Lovelace.

Misses J. White, D. Conibeer, Q. Bale, S. Burnett, M. Barker.

Messrs. H. Parkington, G. Weston, J. Strong.

Hon. Treasurer: Mr. H. Armstrong.

Hon. Secretary: Mr. L. A. Lang

This Programme entitles the holder to free admission on one night only, except Monday

Souvenir Programme—1/-

Cox. Williton

FRIDAY, JUNE 22nd.

PAGEANT OF WILLITON

RECREATION GROUND ... Commence at 7 p.m.

Chairman: G. C. Wyndham, Esq.

Scene 1.—St. Decuman.
,, 2.—The Invasion by the Danes and the fight at Battlegore.
,, 3.—Murder of Beckett.
,, 4.—Sacking of Cleeve Abbey.
,, 5.—Drake and Elizabeth Sydenham.
,, 6.—Mother Shipton.
,, 7.—The Court Leet (by permission of G. C. Wyndham and G. Hinton, Esqs.).
,, 8.—Fire Brigades.
,, 9.—P.T. Display.

Come and see local History re-enacted.

Admission, 6d; Children, 3d.

Players drawn from the Brownies, Guides, Cubs, Scouts, and the School.

Pageant Master: Mr. W. J. White.

SATURDAY, JUNE 23rd.

CHILDREN'S SPORTS MEETING

RECREATION GROUND ... ... Commence 2 o'clock

Flat Races for all ages. Obstacle Races.
Novelty Races. Cycling Races.
Tiny Tots Races.

Admission, 6d.; Children, 3d.

GRAND FIFTY-FIFTY DANCE

CHURCH ROOM ... ... 7.30-11.45 p.m.

Dancing to Mrs. Bryant's Music. Admission, 1s. 6d.

M.C.: Mr. D. Gibbons.

Refreshments; Mrs. Burnell and Mrs. Besley

The Mikado, *performed by Williton Secondary School in the 1960s. Left to right: A Somerfield (Pooh-Bah), T. Barton (Petti-Sing), R. Clavey (Ko-Ko), D. Allen (Pish-Tush), P. Selman (Nanki Poo), G. Bellamy (Yum-Yum), Mr L.A. Witham (Mikado), P. Steer (Katisha).*

ENTERTAINMENT

The remarkable theatrical and musical talents of two Williton teachers, David Beach and John Holroyd, were made evident by the response of a packed and very enthusiastic audience when their production of the musical *Sherana* was performed in 1967. The following is an excerpt from Jack Hurley's review in the *Free Press* of February 11 1967:

The second musical presented by the Williton Players written by David Beach (book and lyrics) and John Holroyd (music), who were responsible for 'Transatlantica' *a few years ago, went off like a star shell, leaving well over 1,000 people with weekend memories of an eyeful of glitter and pains of laughter under the heart.*

'Sherana' *was a sell-out at the Williton Secondary School on the nights of Thursday, Friday and Saturday; never before have the Players enjoyed such support. It was the perfect response to the 'egging on' of Messrs Beach and Holroyd to follow* 'Transatlantica' *with another musical, and with* 'Sherana' *more than two hours of merry nonsense, romance and entanglement about oil concessions it was a huge success. Lee Ackland, whose singing is a delight, had the lead as Sherana, the precocious daughter of a Sheikh, and the Sheikh himself was delivered with pompous dignity by Harry Armstrong. Voiceless but menacing, Laurie Wilson was on stage most of the time as the Nubian Slave. A remarkable show, involving months in writing and producing, which revealed John Holroyd's versatility of style and David Beach's clever lyrics to seal it all off.*

WILLITON PLAYERS

SHERANA

JOHN HOLROYD AND DAVID BEACH

PROGRAMME

A new Musical Comedy performed for the first time at

WILLITON COUNTY SECONDARY SCHOOL

Thursday	Friday	Saturday
Feb. 2nd	Feb. 3rd	Feb. 4th

1967

Above left and above: *The programme for* Sherana *and Williton schoolmaster David Beach, thespian and lyric writer.*

Williton and Watchet based Four Aces Dance Band. The two ladies are Mary Ashman (front) and Peggy Stone (with accordion).

The Four Aces were in popular demand in the late 1940s and they played at venues around the district. The event pictured was at the Regal Ballroom, Minehead (c.1948).

Above: *Fancy dress at a dance at the Church Room, 1950s.*

Left: *Guides' and Brownies' concert in the Church Room, 1950s.*

Right: *Harvest Supper in the Church Room, c.1956.*

A Williton Men's Club dinner at the Egremont Hotel, 1946, at which the lone lady on the left is Mrs Crouch, the landlady; and an unidentified event of 1938.

1923.

WILLITON AND DISTRICT HORTICULTURAL AND COTTAGE GARDENING ASSOCIATION.

THE THIRTEENTH ANNUAL

Flower Show

Will be held at

— WILLITON, —

In a Field kindly lent by Mr. A. W. Hosegood,

On Wednesday, 1st August.

A BAND WILL BE IN ATTENDANCE.

ADMISSION :—2 p.m. to 6 p.m., 1/3; after 6 p.m., 8d. (All prices including Tax). Children, Half-price.

Schedules of Prizes, Entry Forms, Rules and Regulations, can be obtained from - - -

S. L. ROGERS and T. L. SPARKS, Hon. Secs., Williton.

Cox, Printers, Williton and Minehead.

1929. 1929.

WILLITON AND DISTRICT HORTICULTURAL AND COTTAGE GARDENING ASSOCIATION

THE NINETEENTH ANNUAL

Flower Show

Will be held in the

RECREATION GROUND, WILLITON,

Wednesday, July 24th.

A BAND WILL BE IN ATTENDANCE

For Admission, &c., see Posters issued before the Show.

Schedules of Prizes, Entry Forms, Rules and Regulations, can be obtained from:—

S. L. ROGERS and T. L. SPARKS, Hon. Secs., WILLITON.

Cox, Sons, & Co., Ltd., Printers, Williton and Minehead.

Centre: *This flower show illustrated on a postcard of 1908 was held in the field which used to exist behind Doveton House. Before the advent of the Memorial Ground the annual event was held at various suitable sites, among them the field owned by Mr Hosegood, as illustrated by the programme for 1923.*

Bottom: *This is the 1907 Flower Show but the location has not been identified.*

Left and below: *Two other events photographed in the early 1900s were sales of work. The picture on the left is of one such event at the White House, c.1915.*

Right: *Sale of work at Eastfield in 1911.*

Left: *Eastfield House tenants and staff, 1920s. In lorry (from left: Herbert Holcombe, Miss Ellen Heathcote, Miss Webb, Miss Cissy Heathcote, Teddy Holcombe, Henry Date. Standing: Sid Bellamy.*

Below: *An unidentified event, with all dressed smartly, c.1910.*

'Dairymaid' which took 1st prize at Williton Carnival, 1910.

The circus comes to Williton. At the front of this group in Fore Street is B. Gliddon.

CHAPTER THIRTEEN

Local Characters & Tales of Old

THE LATE JACK HURLEY, MBE

Jack Hurley served for over 50 years on the *West Somerset Free Press,* first as a junior reporter in 1930 and rising to be editor at the end of his journalistic career there. Jack was a friendly, understanding man, and who will ever forget the remarkable character he created in Will Widden? Will was always to be found at the foot of Jack's well-read weekly column 'Notes by the Way'. Many readers looked first at the back page of the *Free Press* to see what Will and his cronies had been up to that particular week.

Born in 1913 at Williton, which was always to be his home, Jack went from the village school to Huish's Grammar School, Taunton. As well as his journalistic pieces, he was also the author of several books, notably *Rattle His Bones*, an account of the old Workhouse days at Williton, and of the popular *Murder and Mystery on Exmoor* – amongst others. Jack lived just across the road from the *Free Press* works in North Street, Williton, and his other great interest was music, being organist at Williton Methodist Church for several years. Although an extremely busy man, Jack's office door was always open to all, no matter of what standing, and he would inevitably find time for a chat with his many friends in Williton and throughout West Somerset. For his outstanding service to journalism, Jack was deservedly honoured by Her Majesty the Queen with the award of the MBE after his retirement – a fitting reward for a true Williton worthy and a gentleman. Jack died on 2 December 1983, aged 70 years.

Other Williton worthies to be awarded the MBE include the late Jack Burge (for services to Colonial Police), Frank Morgan (for service to the community) and David Sully (for services to the Fire Brigade).

THE LATE CHARLIE MARTIN

The late Charlie Martin was well known to most villagers both as a businessman and a very friendly and likeable person, often seen in his shop or in the nursery garden in Station Road. It seems that 1983 was a notable year for Charlie, for it was then that he purchased premises in Fore Street to continue the business of greengrocer under the name of J. Jones and Sons, which had previously traded from Robert Street premises, now used as a car accessory shop.

A national Garden of the Year competition (also in 1983) prompted the following press report:

SIGHTSEERS on the West Somerset Railway have been admiring Charlie Martin's back garden for years. Before that passengers on British Rail and the Great Western Railway considered it a bright spot on their travels. For the novel Victorian parterre with box hedges and bedding plants has been catching the public eye for 117 years. Now the judges in a national Garden of the Year contest have voted it the top special prize. Said chief judge and gardening expert Mr. Clay Jones, "One cannot deny that this is special. All the judges agreed they had never, ever, seen anything quite like this little garden".

The garden lies on the opposite side of the railway line to Williton station at Charlie's Highbridge House home. He has been tending the neat collection

Charlie Martin, who passed away on 5 May 2001, aged 86, leaving a notable gap in village life.

of small box hedges and bedding plants since 1931. Before that his great uncle Charlie cared for it after it had been devised by his father John Jones.

Said 68-year-old Charlie, who still carries on the family nursery business begun between 1811 and 1821: "You're supposed to walk through each path without going down any of them twice. I can't reckon up the hours spent on maintaining the garden every year – it comes to a lot. It's the first time I have ever entered a competition and I suppose it will be the last.

"My forebears created the Victorian parterre. I have no intention of letting it lapse. In fact, I feel duty bound to keep it going. And I take great delight in people looking over and admiring it.

"It's just great that it has won national recognition too."

Charlie varies the planting a little from year to year. This year the garden is planted with pelargoniums, ageratum and other bedding plants. Sometimes there are polyanthus for a spring flowering.

WILLIAM COLES

by the late Jack Hurley (1960s)

One of the most unusual obituary notices ever to appear in a newspaper was surely bestowed on the *West Somerset Free Press* in 1899 upon a local character of note named William Coles. Popularly known in the locality simply as 'Miser', few men can have received an obituary amounting to a long and solemn catalogue of their misdeeds, but this was Miser's distinction in print. Indeed, little else could be written of a man who had spent an aggregate of about 20 years in gaol. But as a character, albeit a naughty one, Miser could not be passed over at the end.

How Miser came by his nickname is not clear. Perhaps it was because he lived what was known as 'close'. He was secretive about his movements, and with good reason. For Miser was a thief. Yet that statement needs qualification.

He was not a vicious man, nor a general thief in the sense of the man who is light-fingered with any sort of property belonging to someone else. No, Miser's sole, desperate and unconquerable weakness was for the taste of a fowl, and in the course of a fantastic career as a raider of hen-roosts he put the foxes to shame.

An 'all too sharp fellow' was one description of him. On one of Miser's very numerous appearances in court the chairman remarked: 'You incorrigible rascal. If I had my way I would banish you to the Rock of Gibraltar'. 'Then sir', replied Miser, 'I would bring 'ee back a ring-tailed monkey.'

BUCKET FOR THE STEWING

On his own admission Miser had taken hundreds of birds. He liked to stew them with sage, onions and potatoes, then hold his feast in a field. His stewing utensil was a bucket, and it is significant that on many of the occasions when he appeared in court he was charged with bucket as well as with fowl stealing!

Miser's virtue was to know his own weakness. As far as can be ascertained he never stole anything but fowls and the buckets in which to stew them. Once when a Williton resident offered to give him a labouring job, Miser replied: 'Thankee maister but for God's sake don't put me near your fowls for I shall have to take 'em!'

Stealing is stealing, be it a pin or a pound, a fowl or a fur coat, a bucket or bicycle, yet it is impossible to look back on Miser with the same disapproving eye one might reserve for certain hardened types of criminals. There is reason to believe that Miser was accepted as a character, and that people also accepted, with a kind of resignation, his inevitable misdeeds in the hen houses.

In the middle of the 20th century it is difficult to believe that a man could have spent upwards of 20 years behind bars, for offences that never went beyond fowl and bucket stealing. The changes in judiciary outlook upon offenders have been very great since Miser's day, and one wonders what 20th-century treatment, psychiatry and probation might have done to check Miser in his peregrinations and peculations. It is on record that Miser was a quiet character and well disposed – except toward the hen-roosts. By 1860 when his offences began to get newspaper publicity, he had been in front of the magistrates many times, and had been gaoled for periods varying between 14 days and 12 months. Every time a fowl disappeared, Miser's name was linked with it, but sometimes the complainants remembered that he was already behind bars! So the vanished fowls fell into three groups – those Miser stole, those someone else stole while he was in gaol, and those Miser stole without being found out.

Towards the end of his career he boasted to the Williton police, 'I've had hundreds you don't know about.' At that stage it did not much matter. The police had already booked him enough times in any event. In 1860 it became evident to the magistrates that their sentences on Miser were having no effect, and the next time he came up they remitted him to Quarter Sessions for trial. In January 1861, the higher court gave him six years penal servitude. He came out in 1867 and went straight back for seven years – he had celebrated his release by appropriating a bucket for another stew! And so it went on.

The years of incarceration must have been purgatory in the extreme to a man whose longing for the taste of fowl flesh were akin to those of a drug addict. And so Miser's first act upon release was to start the vicious circle of stewed fowl and prison all over again.

GOOSE FOR A CHANGE

It is hard not to smile when considering the circumstances that led to Miser's first sentence of penal servitude. Christmas was approaching, so who could blame him for upgrading his taste from fowl to goose? He knew where a luscious bird was to be had – on the Countess of Egremont's land. He caught and dispatched the goose, but did not take it away there and then. He hid it in the copse at Burrough's Rocks on the Williton-Stream road. Unfortunately for Miser there was a heavy snowfall in which he left his footprints. Thomas Gould, the Countess of Egremont's under keeper, saw the prints and soon found the goose. Constable Dove was informed, and it was only a question of waiting for Miser to come for his prize. Dove hid himself in the copse, and in due course Miser was nabbed in the very act of collecting. He made a bolt for it but Dove caught him. Miser thought himself particularly unlucky to have had Dove on his heels, for he said to him: 'If it had been George Parsons or Jack Cridland they wouldn't have caught me.' Miser evidently knew, too, that this time the magistrates would send him to a higher court, and he remarked: 'This time I'm done for. This is the best catch that ever I was caught for in my life.' He knew that quite a number of years would pass before he tasted goose for Christmas.

Swift arrest had often been Miser's lot. On numerous occasions the police had come upon him with his fowl and onions already prepared in the bucket, and Miser complained bitterly that he was not allowed to cook and eat the feast before being taken away. His last prison sentence would have ended in 1900, but he came out early as the result of good conduct. This time he did not go straight to a hen-roost. In fact, Miser had stolen his last bird. Prison life, plus his own mode of living when out (he often slept 'rough') had taken toll of his constitution. He reported himself to the police regularly, as he was required to do, and finally, becoming too ill to get about, he entered the Williton Workhouse infirmary. In a few weeks bronchitis had carried Miser off. Henceforth the people would be unable to blame him for lost fowls. When it happened they would say: 'Can't be Miser; he's gone'. But they seemed puzzled. Perhaps they thought Miser's ghost was active!

St Decuman's Church. **(Courtesy James Date Archive)**

NURSE HAKE

by the late Jack Hurley (1960s)

Shutgate (or North-Street), Williton, sees more coffins than does any other highway in the place. It is the last way out for Willitonians on the journey to St Decuman's. And every coffin that goes by is preceded by the spirits of the departed.

Well, that was the view expressed by 'Nurse' Hake. If she claimed extra-sensory powers it was probably due to the fact that she had seen more dead people than anybody else in Williton. But she had experienced happier tasks than that of death-bed watcher. She also came in at the other end as mid-wife for the great event of birth. She may not have regarded every birth as a blessing, though. The times were hard in many a cottage home, and a new baby, who might well be the ninth or tenth, could make those times stiffer still. But Mrs Hake or 'Nurse' Hake, as she was unofficially styled, did her best to bring them all safely into the world. A large number must be walking the streets of Williton today though 'getting a little upward'.

The woman who ushered them into the world was born in 1832, and she died in 1921. She was the 'wise woman' of Williton. She was born before the necessity of nursing qualifications by examination, but possessed natural, innate qualifications. Wise in the matters of life and death, she gave her time and help unstintingly to the people who sent for her, doing what she could to ease the pains of birth and the pangs of death

OLD SCENES

As a young girl Nurse Hake knew a Williton that has disappeared. She had seen the coaches draw up outside the Coach and Horses Inn (now the Egremont Hotel). She had peeped through the door of the Round House next to the inn, and had seen the vagrants lying on their beds of straw. She saw the village girls deck themselves with flowers on May Day and dance in front of the houses. She remembered the awful tragedy at Doniford when three of Mrs Cape's six children were cut off by the tide at Lilley Point and drowned. She knew the factory at Doniford where the blankets for the 'second poor' were made.

SUPERSTITION

Nurse Hake belonged to an age when superstition was still rife, and she was a subscriber to it. She could tell you how 'stars break' on your shoulder when a dear one is about to die, and that angel singing is heard. She could tell you that people's eye strings break just before they die, so that they can see nothing. Thus it was that a dying woman had this to say to old parson Heathcote as he uttered the last prayers: 'I can't see you, but I know you. You are Parson Heathcote, a very good man to them you take to.'

Nurse Hake had a wholesome respect for an old woman who lived at Highbridge, and who excercised strange powers. For instance, there was the business of the everlasting farthing. The old woman would give a child a farthing for running an errand, but the child never got home with it. Somehow the coin always got lost. One bright child decided to put a mark upon a farthing the old woman had given her. Sure enough she lost it. The next day she did another errand, and the old woman gave her a farthing. It was the one the child had marked the day before. Nurse Hake as a young girl had had her own awesome experience of the old woman's powers. She had gone to a stream to fetch a pitcher of water for the old woman, but as fast as she put the water in, out it ran. The old woman feigned a rage, and said Nurse Hake must have broken the pitcher. Nurse Hake, to sooth her, promised to buy another, but she forgot and went home to her dinner. But she felt something queer happening to her. Her dinner fork, when she raised it to her mouth, turned aside, and the food fell off.

Not a bite or drink could the girl take, and she new the old woman must be 'putting the influence upon her'. She went out and bought the old woman a new pitcher. At once the girl felt better, and when she got home was able to eat her food. The episode increased her belief in certain folk having strange powers.

Nurse Hake served Williton well, and when she died the *Free Press*, on behalf of the people, paid tribute to her work. On a day in March it became the turn of the spirit of Nurse Hake to precede her coffin down Shutgate Street and up the hill to St Decuman's, and a page of old Williton was closed. Less would be known of that page had not Nurse Hake talked one day to a man who had always a receptive ear for the reminiscences of old folk – the late Mr Clement Kille.

This photograph comes from David Gliddon and is thought to be the old village pound. Perhaps readers can verify this?

TALES OF OLD

Folklore and legend abound in Somerset and many tales relating to the Williton area have been incorporated into publications covering a wide area of Somerset. Some of the tales are accompanied by photographs taken by H.H. Hole of Williton and are included in these extracts.

BARDON MANOR

The Leigh family had been occupants of Bardon House for a very long time, but when it passed into the ownership of a Robert Leigh in or about 1830 he decided to inquire into the stories about a single white dove and an attic window. The stories related to the persistent breaking of the glass in a small attic window situated in the gable of the building. Having failed to solve the mystery of why the dove would fly at and break the glass, Mr Leigh had the attic cleared and amongst its limited contents a parcel was found labelled 'Concerning the Queen of Scottes'. The papers in the parcel concerned the trial of Mary Queen of Scots and showed the relations between Queen Elizabeth I and Mary when the latter had virtually become a prisoner in England in 1568. They also gave an insight into the Babington Plot against the life of Elizabeth and were presented in a way that influenced Mary. Although denying the allegations she was executed in 1587. The documents were of great historical value and are reported as being catalogued in the British Museum as Egerton Manuscripts 2124. A play, entitled *The White Dove of Bardon*, was written by the late Miss Phöebe Rees, well-known local playwright, and broadcast on BBC radio.

Besides the white dove legend, Bardon has been well-known amongst locals for its ghostly goings-on. One such occurrence has been the sound of the Bardon coach and horses on the gravel drive on a clear, frosty winter's night, but there was never any sighting. Another tradition is that one of the Leighs has been a wanderer in the grounds, carrying a head (not his own) under his arm. Music has been heard in the house, as from a spinet or a harpsichord, said to be coming from a white-haired lady who is wont to flit through the rooms in a dress of rustling silk. Locals would never linger in the vicinity of Bardon after dark and their step would quicken when passing the entrance of the drive.

It is said that the Bardon spirits were exorcised early in the 19th century by seven parsons with bell, book and candle, and that the parsons caused the spirits to take the form of a black dog. This exorcism proved to be none too successful as it is claimed that the said dog appeared many years later.

Bardon still has its reputation for ghosts, and TV cameras have even been used in an attempt to capture them – without success!

Bardon Manor

Cleeve Abbey. (Courtesy James Date Archive)

Combe Sydenham Manor.

Not a Tall Story

An area extending from North Devon over Exmoor and throughout West Somerset is regarded as true Pixie land and some distinguished journalists have given time to consider the origins of Pixie legends. Perhaps the most appealing idea (as recorded by the late Jack Hurley) is that the little folk sprang from angels who were not good enough for Heaven but not bad enough for Hell:

We were not good enough for Heaven,
Not bad enough for Hell,
And therefore unto us given
Unseen on earth to dwell.

Some tales suggest that the little people have been seen and that this has been to the detriment of those who told of the siting, and in the 20th century the residents of the pixie mound near Stogursey were blamed for delays in completion of Hinkley Point power station. Pranks played on isolated victims are said to be the pixies' favourite sport, which only comes to an end if the victim turns his clothes inside out.

Buried Treasure

An early-19th-century search for treasure at Cleeve Abbey led by a farmer exposed a chest thought to contain treasure hidden by the abbot before he left. The farmer was then possessed by selfish desires to keep the treasure to himself and ordered a stop to the dig for refreshment. Strong local cider was then provided for the men to make them drunk and send them to sleep, so that the farmer could examine the contents on his own; however, this was not to be because the central tower of the abbey collapsed and concealed the chest forever.

Saint Decuman

St Decuman is alleged to have arrived at Watchet as a missionary, having crossed the Channel on a raft from Wales accompanied by a cow. He was not well received by heathen men who cut off his head, but unperturbed he washed the wound in St Decuman's Well and put it back on again! St Decuman's name was given to Watchet Church (the mother church of Williton).

The Flat Holm Connection

Words spoken by King Henry II when enraged by reports indicating the popularity of Archbishop Becket of Canterbury are said to have led to the murder of the Archbishop by four knights. The knights were led by Reginald Fitz Urse, who had spent some

Woodspring Priory.

of his boyhood living in the manor house near the site of the present Williton Church. Little seems to be known of the four knights after they were said to have sought forgiveness from the Pope in Rome, but suggestion has been made that Reginald spent the end of his time hidden away at Worspring (Woodspring) Monastery built by his grandson, although he was buried alongside another of the four murderers on the island of Flat Holm.

Combe Sydenham

Tales of Sydenham have lasted since the reign of Elizabeth I when the manor house was built by Sir George Sydenham. It has been recorded that Sir George, a high Sheriff of Somerset, was blessed with another Elizabeth, his beautiful daughter, who was in love with Sir Francis Drake. It was the wish of Sir George that she should marry Sir William Courtenay and although Elizabeth resisted his wishes for some time, following a long absence of Sir Francis Drake she eventually agreed and preparations were made. Arriving at the church a cannonball landed at her feet and, thinking it to be a warning fired by Sir Francis not to marry Sir William, she fled. Elizabeth eventually married Sir Francis and later after his death she married Sir William. The canonball resides at Combe Sydenham house.

Top: *Calling at Nether Stowey en route, c.1840.*
Above: *The post van at Williton, c.1905.*
Right: *Mr Hunt, the postman, with his wife.*

Chapter Fourteen

Then & Now

Some people think that olden times were dull as dull could be,
But things that matter were the same, at
least it seems to me,
No motorcar or phones were there,
no aeroplanes were seen,
But folk were just as happy then, the meadows
just as green,
And hearts were just as brave my boys, the faces just as fair,
The sinners just as plentiful, the saints - well just as rare,
The sun was just as bright my lads and love was just as sweet,
The same old stars were winking when the sweethearts
used to meet,
The flowers were just as fragrant, just as beautiful the snow,
And the Kiddies! how they loved it, in the days of long ago,
The north wind bit as fiercely, and she sang the self same tune,
The skylark loved the sunshine, the nightingale the moon,
The mothers were as patient and unselfish as to-day,
And Father Time as busy tinting mother's hair with grey,
Ah! and the route to Heaven is still the same old way,
Just keep the 'Trail of Kindness' and you'll get there one day.

Anon

The Post Office in Fore Street, 1929.

Top: *Fire brigade with their Merryweather engine, early 1900s.*
Above: *A crew from the early 1900s.*

Main: *The Court, North Street, in the 1920s.*
Inset: *The Square, as it is now known, in 2001.*

Parsons and Hann, c.1920, which is now The County Stores.

This postcard from Judges of Hastings is postmarked 21 August 1914 and was sent to a Mrs Woolehouse in Torquay. It depicts Bellamy's shop complete with wall-mounted Thristle clock. The message reads: 'Got here yesterday, driving and train. Walk to Nether Stowey today.'

Bellamy's Corner shortly before it was demolished in the 1930s.

Hay on the move in North Street, 1930.

North Street, 2000.

Williton Railway Station, October 1924 .

Williton Railway Station, October 2000.

Wyndham Arms Hotel, c.1930.

Wyndham Arms Hotel, 2000.

A Note on Thomas Hawkes

Notes taken from early records indicate that Thomas Hawkes (senr) was born at Wiveliscombe in 1786 and that in 1820 he became licensed as an auctioneer and set up the business Thomas Hawkes & Co., Auctioneers and Valuers, based in Williton. Until 1844 an auctioneer's licence cost £5 with a requirement to pay sixpence in the pound duty on sales, but in 1844 the fee was increased to £10 and duty abolished, which led to an increase in auction sales. From 1826 Mr Hawkes became resident at The Limes (Dovetons), Williton.

Mr T. Hawkes (junr) was born in Williton in 1821, one of a family of ten – five brothers and five sisters – and attended schools in Watchet and Williton. At the age of 13 he was sent to Kentisbeare in Devon, where he attended the school of a Mr Dennis, who set high standards in penmanship, which met the approval of the boy's father. Leaving school at about 14 years of age, T. Hawkes (junr) joined his father's office. By the time of his 18th birthday the demand for land surveyors had increased considerably. He became licensed as an auctioneer in 1847 and the business was from then on known as Hawkes & Son, Land Agents, Surveyors and Auctioneers.

Mr T. Hawkes (senr) died in 1857. By the nature of the business many clients were landowners and farmers, and as a result of these connections Mr T. Hawkes entered a partnership with Mr J. Risdon, a relation by marriage. This partnership was set up as Hawkes & Risdon for 'the sale of real and personal

Mr T. Hawkes (senr) at home at Dovetons. Later a forester named Andrew Webber lived here. He travelled to his clients (among them Lady Lovelace of Ashley Combe, Porlock) by motorcycle and side-car.

property for probate and composition' (although it did not encompass surveying or valuations).

With the passage of time the business became very successful. The Williton monthly auctions commenced in 1866. In 1889, following changes of residence, Mr J. Risdon (junr) and Mr H. Andrew (nephew of T. Hawkes) were made partners in the firm, which became known as Hawkes, Risdon & Andrew until July 1896 when Mr Thomas Hawkes retired from this firm. Mr H. Andrew left Williton and the partnership in 1903, and from this time the two Risdons traded separately as J. Risdon & Son. Mr A.W. Hosegood (an assistant) was then licensed as an auctioneer associated with Thomas Hawkes and trading continued as T. Hawkes & Co., Auctioneers & Valuers. After a period of very successful business Mr Hosegood was taken ill and relinquished his auctioneer's licence. In 1905 the auction mart was taken over by John Risdon & Son.

Mr Thomas Hawkes (junr), who never married, died in June 1906 in his 86th year; he was one of the best-known professional men in West Somerset. His first three journeys to London from Williton were accomplished entirely by horse-drawn coach. In his earlier life he was closely associated with the improvements that set in with respect to road-making, main roads in those days being managed by turnpike trusts. He had also, when a young man, a good deal to do with surveying for railroads, especially in the Midlands.

Mr Hawkes took much interest in all matters connected with Williton and the immediate neighbourhood. For a great many years he was treasurer for the Williton and Dunster Association and of the Loyal St Decuman's Lodge of the Independent Order of Oddfellows, a friendly society.

He took a great interest in the building of the Wesleyan Chapel (Methodist Church), Sunday School and ancillary buildings (now converted into dwellings), and Manse at Williton, being treasurer to the building fund. All musical matters had his keen sympathy and interest, and during the many years of the existence of the Williton Choral Class and Orchestra, he was invariably Chairman at the concerts which they rendered.

Mr Hawkes and his father were closely associated with Williton life for over 109 years.

'Long Tom' Hosegood (left), who was Chairman of the Rural District Council and farmed at Aller Farm. He is pictured here with Arthur Stoate, who farmed the neighbouring Bridge Farm. Long Tom had five sons and a daughter, Muriel. The sons included Archie, who was killed during the First World War carrying cigarettes to his comrades; Bernard, who farmed at Bratton Court, Minehead; Leonard, who emigrated to Australia; Harry, who became a solicitor and founded the business of Hosegood Burgess (which his son, Tom, eventually joined, also serving in the Middle East during the Second World War); and Gordon, who farmed at Aller before dying young. Muriel then took on the tenancy of the farm with her husband, the auctioneer George Culverwell, remaining until the late 1960s.

Subscribers

Timothy J. Ackland, Ballinabarny, Eire
Alicia M. Ackland, Minehead, Somerset
Revd Richard Allen, Williton, Somerset
Tessa S. Appleby, Cottiford, Williton, Somerset
Oliver G. D. Appleby, Cottiford, Williton, Somerset
Susan Appleby, Cottiford, Williton, Somerset
Betty and Peter Armstrong, Taunton, Somerset
Phyl Ashman, Williton, Somerset
Mr Malcolm Ashman, Williton, Somerset
Ian Barratt
Linda J. Barrell, Taunton, Somerset
David and Pamela Beach, Williton, Somerset
David W. Beach, Williton, Somerset
Janet R. Beaver, Williton, Somerset
P. G. Berry, Williton, Somerset
Eric Bird, Paignton, Devon
Ann and Keith Bishop, Williton, Somerset
Roger and Tracey-Ann Biss, Williton, Somerset
Harry Bowles MBE, Shepton Mallet, Somerset
Ray Braunton, Wellington, Shropshire
Gordon and Pat Bryant, Williton, Somerset
David and Dilys Bryant, Watchet, Somerset
Valerie J. Buller, Williton, Somerset
Anne D. Buller, Twickenham, Middlesex
Mr and Mrs J. Carslake, Williton, Somerset
Betty Cavill, Williton, Somerset
Rodney M. Challands, Portishead, North Somerset
Station Officer Richard Chamberlain, Williton Fire Station
Barbara M. Chapman, Grantham/ formerly of Williton
Michael Chapman, Yeovil, Somerset
Violet Chibbett, Williton, Somerset
Maurice and Joyce Chidgey, Watchet, Somerset
Mrs Phyllis M. Chidgey, Williton, Somerset
Mr and Mrs B. A. Chilcott, Williton, Somerset
Len and Dot Chorley, Williton, Somerset
Laurence R. Chorley, Alcombe, Minehead, Somerset
Jean Claris
Adrian D. Clark, Williton, Somerset
Martin J. Codrington and Laura J. Pike, Wayside, Williton, Somerset
Peter Coldicutt, Gloucestershire
I. K. Coleby, Taunton, Somerset
Norman Coles, Westonzoyland, Somerset
Mary Coles, Doniford Road, Williton, Somerset
Joan Collins, Penarth
David Cooke, Williton, Somerset
Teresa and Ray Cooke, Williton, Somerset

Sandra E. A. Coombs, Williton, Somerset
Joan I. Cordingley, Williton, Somerset
Ken and Jean Craswell, North Street, Williton, Somerset
Major John F. Cridge, Williton, Somerset
Colin J. Curling and Patricia N. Grocock, Alcombe, Minehead, Somerset
Danesfield C of E Community Middle School, Williton, Somerset
H. and D. Davis, Minehead, Somerset
Roger and Rosemary Davis, Williton, Somerset
Don Dee, Williton, Somerset
B. F. Dennett, Williton, Somerset
Mrs Annette Dickinson, Torquay, Devon
Sue and David Drabble, Sampford Brett
Robert Dupree, Weymouth, Dorset
Beryl A. Dyer, Williton, Somerset
Joan Edwards, Williton, Somerset
Mr P. D. Edwards, Old Cleeve, Somerset
Molly P. Farmer
Keith and Brenda Foster, Williton, Somerset
Sue and Tony Gay, Doniford Meadow
Joan and Geoff Gilham, Williton, Somerset
A. M. and J. F. Girard, France
A. T. Goble, Williton, Somerset
Margaret Gould, Dunster, Somerset
Dr John Greed, Portishead
George Haller, Crowcombe, Somerset
Mrs J. S. Hammill, Williton, Somerset
Kenneth S. Harris, Williton, Somerset
James A. Hendrick, St Audries, Williton, Somerset
Mr John Hesford, Williton, Somerset
Peter Hill, Doniford Road, Williton, Somerset
Dr Rebecca Hobbs, Flaxpool, Somerset
D. B. Hosegood, Williton, Somerset
Michael Howe, Williton, Somerset
Mr Craig Howells, Watchet, Somerset
Roy and Janet Howells, Williton, Somerset
Wendy M. Hubbard, Conington, Peterborough
F. J. Hutchings, Williton Meat Supply
Violet M. James, Minehead, Somerset
John Jenkins, formerly of Sampford Brett, Williton, Somerset
F. D. J. Johnson OBE, Woolston, County Surveryor Somerset 1975–1990
M. H. Jones, Taunton, Somerset
Sue and Charlie Knight, Williton, Somerset
David J. Langdon, Williton, Somerset
Michael Leavy, Vancouver Island, Canada
Janet E. Lee, Williton, Somerset
George and Ann Lewis, Williton, Somerset
Mrs Elizabeth Grace Lewis, Williton, Somerset
Percy and Stella Long, Williton, Somerset
Carole P. Mackereth, Dulverton, Somerset
Thomas H. Mallett, Williton, Somerset
Bryan Mason, Williton, Somerset
Ken and Doreen Matthews, Williton, Somerset
W. H. K. Mattravers, Williton, Somerset
Marie Breley Milnes (née Gadd), Williton, Somerset
Bob and Val Moore, Williton, Somerset
Frank C. Morgan M.B.E., Williton, Somerset
Judith Nesfield, Williton, Somerset
Rosemary M. Newbold, Minehead, Somerset
Mr and Mrs M. Nicholas, Williton, Somerset
Mr M. Palmer, Dunster, Somerset
Mr R. Palmer, Alcombe, Minehead, Somerset
Mrs Audrey T. Palmer (née Chilcott), Williton, Somerset
Jean Pierre and Christiane Cosse, Neung sur Beuvron
Nigel and Sue Pike, Bilbrook, Somerset
Deane Potter, Orchard Way, Williton, Somerset
Charles W. Pugsley, Somerset
Noel E. C. Pullin, Williton, Somerset

Mr John M. Richards, Williton, Somerset
Valerie Richards, Torweston Farm, Williton, Somerset
Antony G. Rigden, Williton, Somerset
Mark Risdon, Williton, Somerset
Roger Risdon, Williton, Somerset
Anne Roberts, Watchet, Somerset
Mr and Mrs A. G. Rowe, Reed Close, Watchet, Somerset
K. Rufus MCIWEM
D. G. and J. L. Scott, Williton, Somerset
L. T. Scott, Williton, Somerset
C. P. Sharp OBE, Maulden, Beds. (evacuee 1940–41)
Roy Shopland, Westhill, Devon
B. and J. Skudder, Doniford, Somerset
Mark A. Slack, Williton, Somerset
Mary Slade, Williton, Somerset
Jane E. Smith, Oxford
David Sparks, Keynsham, Somerset
Philip Sparks, Nailsea, Somerset
Mr Vivian Spence, Doniford
G. M. Spence, Williton, Somerset
Frank and Doreen Stanford, Williton, Somerset
Donald Stevens, Williton, Somerset
Michael V. Sully, Minehead, Somerset
G. Sully, Williton, Somerset
David W. Sully MBE, Williton, Somerset
Ivor Sutton, formerly of Orchard Mill, Williton
Peter Swann, Doniford House, Jumby Bay, Antigua/Williton 1935
Joyce A. Swann, USA
H. and J. Tennant, Williton, Somerset
Carol and Chris Thompson, Otterhampton, Somerset
Charlie Thomson, Williton, Somerset
Keith, Joy and Zöe Towells, Watchet, Somerset
Mr Reg Trebble, Bridge Street
Chris Trebble, Williton, Somerset
G.C., R. M., D.M., and R.H. Troman, Williton, Somerset
Mrs Alison M. Vaughan, Williton, Somerset
The Veale family, Williton, Somerset
Jo Vincent
John F. W. Walling, Newton Abbot, Devon
John B. Ward
Geoffrey Webber, formerly Williton, Somerset
Malcolm G. Wedlake, Ystrad Mynach, Mid Glamorgan
Geoffrey D. Western, Taunton, Somerset
H. R. White, Liddimore Farm, Watchet, Somerset
Peter M. White, Honiton, Devon
Edith White
Ray and Hazel Whittington, Williton, Somerset
M. B. C. Wicking
Robert John Wilkins, Woolston, Somerset
Joan Williams, Bishops Lydeard, Somerset
Anthony G. Williams, Williton, Somerset
Peter and Anne Williamson, Williton, Somerset
Williton and District Twinning Association
Mrs Stephanie Jayne Woodley, Williton, Somerset
Melanie J. Woollam, Williton, Somerset
Virginia Yandle (née McCord), Sampford Brett, Somerset
Hannah Young, Bicknoller Inn, Nr Williton, Somerset

ALSO AVAILABLE IN THE SERIES

The Book of Addiscombe • Various
Book of Bampton • Caroline Seward
Book of Bickington • Stuart Hands
The Book of Blandford Forum • Various
The Book of Brixham • Frank Pearce
The Parish Book of Cerne Abbas • Vale & Vale
The Book of Chittlehampton • Various
The Book of Constantine • Moore & Trethowan
The Book of Cornwood and Lutton • Various
The Book of Creech St Michael • June Small
The Book of Cullompton • Various
The Book of Grampound with Creed • Bane & Oliver
The Book of Hayling Island and Langstone • Rogers
The Book of Helston • Jenkin with Carter
The Book of Hemyock • Clist & Dracott
The Book of High Bickington • Avril Stone
The Book of Ilsington • Dick Wills
The Book of Lamerton • Ann Cole and Friends
Lanner, A Cornish Mining Parish • Scharron Schwartz & Roger Parker
The Book of Loddiswell • Various
The Book of Lustleigh • Tim Hall
The Book of Manaton • Various
The Book of Meavy • Pauline Hemery
The Book of Morchard Bishop • Jeff Kingaby
Minehead with Alcombe • Binding & Stevens
The Book of North Newton • Robins & Robins
The Book of Pimperne • Compiled by Jean Coull
The Book of Plymtree • Tony Eames
The Book of Porlock • Denis Corner
Postbridge – The Heart of Dartmoor • Reg Bellamy
The Book of Priddy • Various
The Book of Rattery • Various
The Book of South Stoke • Various
South Tawton and South Zeal with Sticklepath • Roy and Ursula Radford
The Book of Sparkwell with Hemerdon and Lee Mill • Pam James
The Book of Stourton Caundle • Philip Knott
The Book of Swanage • Rodney Legg
The Book of Torbay • Frank Pearce
Uncle Tom Cobley and All • Stephen Woods
The Book of Watchet • Compiled by David Banks
The Book of West Huntspill • Various
Widecombe-in-the-Moor • Stephen Woods
Woodbury • Roger Stokes
The Book of Woolmer Green • Various

SOME OF THE MANY FORTHCOMING TITLES

The Book of Addiscombe, Vol. II • Various
The Book of Barnstaple • Avril Stone
The Book of Bridestowe • R. Cann
The Book of Buckland Monochorum • Hemery
The Book of Carshalton • Stella Wilks
The Book of Chagford • Ian Rice
The Book of Chittlehamholt with Warkleigh & Satterleigh • Richard Lethbridge
The Book of Colney Heath • Bryan Lilley
The Book of Down St Mary • Various
The Book of Dulverton with Brushford, Bury & Exebridge • Various
The Book of Dunster • Hilary Binding
The Book of Hurn • Margaret Phipps
The Book of Lulworth • Rodney Legg
The Book of Markyate • Richard Hogg
The Book of Mawnan Smith • Various
The Book of Newdigate • John Callcut
The Book of Newton Abbot • Ian Rice
The Book of North Tawton • Various
The Book of Northlew with Ashbury • Various
The Book of Peter Tavy • Various
The Book of Publow with Pensford • Various
The Book of Sampford Courtenay with Honeychurch • Stephanie Pouya
The Book of Staverton • Pete Lavis
The Book of Studland • Rodney Legg
The Book of Wythall • Val Lewis

For details of any of the above titles or if you are interested in writing your own community history, please contact: Community Histories Editor, Halsgrove House, Lower Moor Way, Tiverton Business Park, Tiverton, Devon EX16 6SS, England, e-mail: naomic@halsgrove.com

In order to include as many historic photographs as possible in this volume, a printed index is not included. However, the Community History Series is currently being indexed by Genuki. For further information and indexes to volumes in the series, please visit: http://www.cs.ncl.ac.uk/genuki/DEV/indexingproject.html